Cambridge Elements ☰

Elements in Applied Linguistics
edited by
Li Wei
University College London
Zhu Hua
University College London

SECOND LANGUAGE PRAGMATICS

Wei Ren
Beihang University

CAMBRIDGE
UNIVERSITY PRESS

CAMBRIDGE
UNIVERSITY PRESS

University Printing House, Cambridge CB2 8BS, United Kingdom

One Liberty Plaza, 20th Floor, New York, NY 10006, USA

477 Williamstown Road, Port Melbourne, VIC 3207, Australia

314–321, 3rd Floor, Plot 3, Splendor Forum, Jasola District Centre,
New Delhi – 110025, India

103 Penang Road, #05–06/07, Visioncrest Commercial, Singapore 238467

Cambridge University Press is part of the University of Cambridge.

It furthers the University's mission by disseminating knowledge in the pursuit of
education, learning, and research at the highest international levels of excellence.

www.cambridge.org
Information on this title: www.cambridge.org/9781009077545
DOI: 10.1017/9781009082709

First published 2022

A catalogue record for this publication is available from the British Library.

ISBN 978-1-009-07754-5 Paperback
ISSN 2633-5069 (online)
ISSN 2633-5050 (print)

Cambridge University Press has no responsibility for the persistence or
accuracy of URLs for external or third-party internet websites referred to
in this publication and does not guarantee that any content on such
websites is, or will remain, accurate or appropriate.

Second Language Pragmatics

Elements in Applied Linguistics

DOI: 10.1017/9781009082709
First published online: July 2022

Wei Ren
Beihang University

Author for correspondence: Wei Ren, weiren@buaa.edu.cn

Abstract: This Element introduces the areas that second language (L2) pragmatics research has investigated. It begins with a theme-based review of the field with respect to L2 pragmatics learning, teaching, and assessing. The section on pragmatics learning examines studies on learners' pragmatic production and perception, and analyzes research modalities in this field. The section on pragmatics teaching examines the effects of and different approaches to L2 pragmatics instruction; and the section on pragmatics assessing examines the aspects involved in testing learners' pragmatic competence, and studies on issues related to validity and rating in pragmatics assessing. The Element then analyzes studies exploring learners' cognitive processes during pragmatic performance, and case studies are provided to showcase two ongoing projects – one investigating advanced learners' self-praise on social media and the other investigating lingua franca pragmatics among children. Finally, the Element offers some topics and questions for future research in L2 pragmatics.

Keywords: second language pragmatics, pragmatic competence, pragmatics learning, pragmatics teaching, pragmatics assessing, cognitive process

ISBNs: 9781009077545 (PB), 9781009082709 (OC)
ISSNs: 2633-5069 (online), 2633-5050 (print)

Contents

1 Second Language Pragmatics: An Introduction

Second language (L2) pragmatics is an interdisciplinary field involving pragmatics and L2 research. Pragmatics is a key domain in linguistics; there are many published definitions, but the most commonly adopted one in L2 pragmatics was provided by Crystal (1997: 301), who defined it as "the study of language from the point of view of users, especially of the choices they make, the constraints they encounter in using language in social interaction and the effects their use of language has on other participants in the act of communication." This definition highlights that both speaker meaning and recipient uptake should be included in pragmatics research (Kasper and Ross, 2013). Pragmatics is generally distinguished into pragmalinguistics and sociopragmatics, with the former addressing the relations between linguistic forms and their function, while the latter addresses the relations between linguistic choices and social constraints (Ren, 2018a). Following the convention in applied linguistics and L2 pragmatics (Kasper and Rose, 2002; Ross and Kasper, 2013; Taguchi and Roever, 2017), in this Element I use L2 as a cover term to refer to an additional language of any status, whether foreign, second, third, fourth, heritage language, or lingua franca.

Second language pragmatics investigates learners' pragmatic competence, which is defined by Thomas (1983: 92) as "the ability to use language effectively in order to achieve a specific purpose and to understand language in context." Although many L2 pragmatics studies have examined pragmatic competence from a stable perspective in terms of individuals' abilities (see reviews in Kasper, 2006; Taguchi, 2017, 2019), Thomas' definition actually points to both speaker and hearer meaning in interaction. Nevertheless, it neglects other semiotic and multimodal resources that are used in interaction, such as emoticons and emojis in digital communication. To reflect this, I propose a downgrading of the language part in Thomas' definition and the addition of an appropriateness dimension, thus defining pragmatic competence as the ability to use linguistic, semiotic, and multimodal resources effectively and appropriately to achieve a communicative purpose, and to understand such uses in interaction. It has to be explained that language is also a semiotic resource, but here I would like to highlight it and therefore use linguistic and semiotic in parallel. I agree with Taguchi (2019) that pragmatic competence is best understood as a multi-dimensional and multi-layered construct that entails three main components: "(1) linguistic and sociocultural knowledge of what forms to use in what context; (2) interactional abilities to use the knowledge in a flexible, adaptive manner corresponding to changing context; and (3) agency to make an informed decision on whether or not to implement the knowledge in

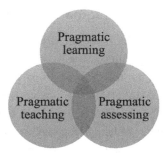

Figure 1 Branches of L2 pragmatics

the community" (Taguchi, 2019: 4). However, I would like to add other semiotic and multimodal knowledge to the first component.

Although many studies focus on acquisitional aspects in L2 pragmatics (e.g., González-Lloret, 2020; Kasper and Rose, 2002; Ren, 2018a), the field is in fact much broader, consisting of pragmatic learning, pragmatic teaching, and pragmatic assessing (see Figure 1).

The main aims of this Element are twofold. First, it will provide an up-to-date overview of the current research on learning, teaching, and assessing L2 pragmatics, as well as learners' cognitive processes during such procedures. However, I do not intend to provide a diachronic overview of the history of the field, but rather to focus on some of its key topics. In addition, when reviewing existing works I have deliberately skewed towards publications in this century. Second, it will explore topics that need particular attention in L2 pragmatics to develop the field both in scope and in depth, in turn to reflect and promote the advancement of its two higher-order fields: pragmatics and L2 research. I also showcase two projects in progress before discussing the future directions and suggestions.

2 Second Language Pragmatics Learning

This section introduces works investigating learners' L2 pragmatic learning, starting with pragmatic production and followed by pragmatic perception. Research modality in L2 pragmatics learning studies is also examined in this section.

2.1 Pragmatic Production

Kasper and Rose (2002: 117) pointed out that L2 pragmatics was "heavily outweighed by the proliferation of studies on pragmatic production." This trend remains and reflects the preference for production in pragmatics in general. The skew towards production is understandable, since production can provide more nuanced and easily observed data than perception, and in many cases production involves perception of the other interlocutor's communication.

Production studies often investigate learners' production across different influential factors, such as L2 proficiency, learning environment (study abroad vs. study at home), and length of stay abroad. They have yielded controversial and sometimes contradictory findings with respect to the impact of the factors on learners' pragmatic production, so that our understanding of the effects of these influential factors is incomplete. For instance, partially because different pragmatic targets are examined in different studies, the findings relating to the association between pragmatic competence and linguistic proficiency are often inconsistent. Although most researchers agree that learners' pragmatic production and their linguistic proficiency do not show a linear correlation, generalization becomes difficult when studies do not employ standardized tests for determining learners' proficiency levels. Another example is the common finding that learners perform differently from native speakers. However, since a study can only focus on a small cohort of participants, it cannot investigate multiple factors that may influence learners' pragmatic learning. Given that the number of influencing factors and the way in which they may interact are often different for different learners, it is very complex to compare the findings. For example, Takahashi and Beebe (1987) found that learners who had studied abroad for an average of four years had a broader range of expressions and more flexibility to adjust their level of directness according to different situations than those who had studied abroad for an average of seven months. Bella (2011) demonstrated that even learners with a 4.5-year residence-abroad experience still displayed an underdeveloped pragmatic ability in relation to mitigation devices. Ren (2019b) found that with respect to request strategies, learners with two years of study-abroad experience resembled native speakers more, while learners with longer study-abroad experience of two to four years showed more non-target-like development. Therefore, this section focuses on what L2 pragmatics production research has investigated, rather than detailed findings in particular areas.

2.1.1 Speech Acts

Second language pragmatics production has mainly investigated speech acts (Bardovi-Harlig, 2005; Kasper and Dahl, 1991; Ren, 2018a). However, this does not mean that speech acts are sufficiently understood. Indeed, only a couple of speech acts have attracted much attention, with many more being only occasionally explored or even neglected altogether.

Requests. Requests are the most widely investigated speech act in L2 pragmatics research. Among the target languages, English is the most frequently examined (e.g., Achiba, 2003; Economidou-Kogetsidis and Woodfield, 2012; Schauer, 2009), receiving much more attention than any other language. Spanish seems to be the second most frequently examined target language (e.g., Czerwionka and Cuza, 2017; Kuriscak, 2015; Shively, 2011), followed by Arabic (e.g., Al Masaeed, 2017; Al-Gahtani and Roever, 2012), Chinese (e.g., Li, 2014; Ren, 2019b), and Greek (e.g., Bella, 2012b; Vassilaki and Selimis, 2020). German (e.g., Barron, 2003; Cunningham, 2017), Japanese (e.g., Taguchi, 2015a), French (e.g., Lundell and Erman, 2012), and Indonesian (e.g., Hassall, 2003) have also been examined in request production studies, but not frequently.

Many studies examine learners from diverse first language (L1) backgrounds. When learners are from a homogenous L1 background, American English learners appear to be the most frequently examined (e.g., Li, 2014; Shively, 2011; Su and Ren, 2017), followed by Japanese learners (e.g., Economidou-Kogetsidis and Halenko, 2022; Taguchi, 2007b; Takahashi, 1996) and Chinese learners (e.g., Li, 2000; Su, 2010). Learners from other languages have also been examined, but less frequently, including Arabic (e.g., Al-Ali and Alawneh, 2010), French (e.g., Béal, 1994), German (e.g., Schauer, 2009), Persian (e.g., Ghavamnia *et al.*, 2012), Serbian (e.g., Savic, 2014), and Swedish (e.g., Lundell and Erman, 2012).

The studies have examined learners' production of request strategies, and their external and internal modification of requests. The most commonly used coding scheme was developed by Blum-Kulka *et al.* (1989) in the well-known Cross-cultural Speech Act Realization Project (CCSARP), although it is often used with adaptations. Request strategies are coded in terms of levels of directness in the head act, which are divided into direct, conventionally indirect, and nonconventionally indirect requests. External and internal modification refer to pragmatic strategies which mitigate or intensify the request but do not in themselves carry the request force, with the former falling out of the head act while the latter within the head act (full details can be found in the CCSARP coding manual in Blum-Kulka *et al.*, 1989).

Refusals. Refusals may be the second most investigated speech act in L2 pragmatics production research, although the number of studies on refusals is much lower than the number on requests. Refusal studies predominantly focus on English as the target language (e.g., Al-Gahtani and Roever, 2018; Ren, 2015; Taguchi, 2013b), with only a few studies investigating other languages such as Arabic (e.g., Morkus, 2021), Greek (e.g., Bella, 2011, 2014b), Hebrew (e.g., Stavans and Webman Shafran, 2018), Chinese (e.g., Hong, 2011), and Spanish (e.g., Félix-Brasdefer, 2003, 2004, 2013).

Studies on L2 refusals often examine learners from homogenous L1 backgrounds, although some studies do include learners with a mixture of L1s (e.g., Bardovi-Harlig and Hartford, 1993). Interestingly, this research shows a different trend from request studies. When English is the target language, Chinese learners are the most frequently examined (e.g., Chang, 2011; Lee, 2016; Ren, 2013), followed by Iranian learners (L1 Persian) (e.g., Allami and Naeimi, 2011; Shishavan and Sharifian, 2013), Saudi Arabic learners (e.g., Al-Gahtani and Roever, 2018), Japanese learners (e.g., Gass and Houck, 1999; Taguchi, 2007b), Javanese learners (e.g., Wijayanto, 2016), and Thai learners (e.g., Wannaruk, 2008). When languages other than English are the focal target languages, the learners are almost always from English-speaking countries.

Most studies investigate refusal strategies and adjuncts to refusals (i.e., external modification), following the coding scheme developed by Beebe *et al.* (1990). Unlike request studies that often analyze internal modification, only a few studies have examined the internal modification of refusals (e.g., Barron, 2003; Bella, 2011; Ren, 2013). This may be due in part to two reasons. On the one hand, the speech act of refusal is often realized in indirect strategies, which increases the difficulties and complexities involved in identifying internal modifiers. On the other hand, there is no well-accepted coding scheme for the internal modifiers of refusals, as there is for studies on requests.

Apology. Apology is another often-examined speech act in L2 pragmatic production, although it is examined much less frequently than requests. Studies in this area either investigate how English L1 speakers apologize in a target language, such as Arabic (e.g., Al Masaeed *et al.*, 2018), German (e.g., Barron, 2019), and Russian (e.g., Shardakova, 2005), or how learners from other languages apologize in English, for example, Catalan learners (e.g., Barón and Ortega, 2018), Chinese learners (e.g., Chang, 2010), Saudi Arabic learners (e.g., El-Dakhs, 2018), and Serbian learners (e.g., Savic, 2014). Only Warga and Schölmberger (2007) diverge from this trend, examining Austrian German learners' apologies in French.

These studies not only investigate learners' apology strategies but also how they upgrade their apologies, based on earlier coding schemes for apologies (e.g., Blum-Kulka *et al.*, 1989; Olshtain, 1989). The notion of the illocutionary force indicating device (IFID) is important for coding apologies, which is the formulaic form containing "the explicit, performative verbs which express an apology" (Olshtain, 1989: 157). The IFID can be strengthened internally by various means such as intensifying adverbials and emotional expressions (see more in the CCSARP coding manual in Blum-Kulka *et al.*, 1989).

Other speech acts. More speech acts have been investigated, but most of them have only been examined sporadically. Many have only been investigated with English as the target language. For example, learners' production of advice/suggestions has been explored in a few studies, all focusing on English (e.g., Bardovi-Harlig and Hartford, 1993). Among these, Chinese learners seem to be the most frequently examined (e.g., Hinkel, 1997; Li, 2010; Taguchi *et al.*, 2021), and Japanese learners have also been studied (e.g., Matsumura, 2001, 2003).

Further speech acts that have been investigated with English and other languages as the target language include complaints (e.g., Nguyen and Pham, 2021; Tatsuki, 2000; Yuan and Zhang, 2018), compliment responses (e.g., Huth, 2006; Shimizu, 2009), criticisms (e.g., Nguyen, 2008, 2017), greeting responses (e.g., Jaworski, 1994; Ying and Ren, 2021), offers (e.g., Bella, 2016), and sympathy after bereavement (e.g., Meiners, 2017). The studies have enlarged our understanding of learners' acquisition of speech acts, addressing the call for investigating more speech acts and expanding the pool of target languages. However, the findings would be more mutually inferable if the studies could be guided by similar frameworks of speech act taxonomy and employ some standardized measurements for determining learners' proficiency. On the other hand, it is beneficial for L2 pragmatics to follow the trend of pragmatics research to investigate speech acts in a bigger picture of interaction in a more dynamic manner. These achieved, L2 pragmatics can draw more robust generalizations and compare its achievement with other branches of pragmatics and L2 research to contribute more to theoretical constructions of the two fields. It is encouraging to see that several studies have explored advanced learners' uses of speech acts to express their identities and enhance their social relations. For example, Habib (2008) examines how four female near-native users of English employ teasing and disagreement to display personal identity, while Ren and Liu (2021) explore how Chinese graduate learners of English express their phatic communion in gratitude emails to professors.

2.1.2 Conventional Expressions

Some studies have investigated learners' production of formulaic expressions. Although different scholars use different terms for these, such as conventional expressions (Bardovi-Harlig, 2009), formulas (Bardovi-Harlig, 2008), and pragmatic routines (Taguchi, 2013a), the terms are often used interchangeably and refer to almost the same concept, that is, of idiomatic multi-word expressions (see Bardovi-Harlig, 2012 for a review of the differences among the terms).

Empirical studies often examine both learners' production and recognition of L2 conventional expressions. Production studies have mostly investigated English conventional expressions, apart from a couple of studies on Chinese (e.g., Bardovi-Harlig and Su, 2018; Taguchi *et al.*, 2013). Although conventional expressions have been discussed in other languages (e.g., Kecskes, 2003), few empirical studies have been conducted.

Production research on conventional expressions generally undergoes two preparatory phases prior to collecting data from learners. In the first phase, researchers select candidate formulaic expressions by various methods, including authentic conversations (Bardovi-Harlig, 2009), field notes (Taguchi *et al.*, 2013), discourse completion tasks (DCTs) (Edmonds, 2014), or textbooks and reference works (Taguchi *et al.*, 2013; Yang, 2016). The candidate expressions are then tested with a group of native speakers to decide the "correct" answer that will be used to test learners. Through this checking process the research establishes criteria for the formulae using a cut-off point. Most research chooses a 50 percent cut-off for native speaker preference (e.g., Bardovi-Harlig, 2009; Bardovi-Harlig and Su, 2018; Taguchi *et al.*, 2013), although Yang (2016) employs a 67 percent cut-off.

2.1.3 Address Terms

Address terms express sociopragmatic values and affect interpersonal relationships. They are often examined as a type of modification in L2 pragmatics research, either as an alerter (e.g., Ren, 2019b; Taguchi *et al.*, 2016b) and attention-getter (Martínez-Flor, 2012), or as a type of internal modifier (Hassall, 2012; Pan, 2012). However, this section focuses on studies taking address terms as their specific research targets.

The production of address terms in L2 has been investigated in a range of languages. The most often examined types are the T/V address forms in French (*tu* vs. *vous*), German (*du* vs. *sie*), and Spanish (*tú* vs. *usted*) (e.g., Blood, 2018; Kinginger and Belz, 2005; Villarreal, 2014). Studies have also examined learner use of address terms in Korean (e.g., Brown, 2013; Kim and Brown, 2014) and Indonesian (e.g., Hassall, 2013). Studies have explored the difficulties of and the study-abroad effect on English learners' use of address forms in another language, with findings generally indicating a positive effect of study abroad and learners' agency in using those address terms (Ishihara, 2019).

2.1.4 Pragmatic Markers

Pragmatic markers have attracted increasing attention in L2 pragmatics research, with researchers investigating the frequency and functions of learners' production of one or a group of pragmatic markers. Not surprisingly, English pragmatic markers constitute the majority of the targets, among which *like* is the most investigated (e.g., Liu, 2016; Magliacane and Howard, 2019), followed by *well, you know,* and *I mean* (e.g., Buysse, 2015; Fernández-Polo, 2014; Wei, 2011). Other English pragmatic markers that have been examined include *so, I don't know, and, just, sort of/kind of, I think, yes/yeah,* and *please* (e.g., Buysse, 2012; Gablasova *et al.*, 2017; Hosoda and Aline, 2022).

Studies have also examined pragmatic markers in L2 Spanish, such as *pues* (close to *well, so, then*) and *bueno* (close to *anyway, okay, so, well*), and the turn-initial discourse markers *y* and *sí* (García García, 2021), Italian, such as *sì (yes, ok), allora (so, then), quindi (then, therefore),* and *dunque (therefore, be, well)* (De Cristofaro and Badan, 2021), and Japanese, such as the contrastive markers *demo, kedo,* and *ga* (all can be translated into English as *but, though, although*) (Geyer, 2007). Chinese markers have also been examined, mostly focusing on utterance-final particles (e.g., Diao, 2016; Diao and Chen, 2021).

2.1.5 Conversation Management

Studies on learners' abilities to manage conversations investigate a range of topics under the framework of conversation analysis (Schegloff, 2007; Sidnell, 2010), such as repair, sequential organization, turn taking, turn design, and preference organization (Kasper and Ross, 2013). For example, Itakura (2002) examines the effect of gender on topic development in informal conversations by Japanese learners of English, Al-Gahtani and Roever (2012) analyze the sequential organizations of requests of Arabic learners of English across four proficiency levels, and Al-Gahtani and Roever (2018) examine preference organization of Arabic learners of English across three proficiency levels. In addition, Savić and Đorđević (2021) investigate relational practices in emails in English by Norwegian speakers.

Languages other than English have also been studied. Guillot (2009, 2012) investigates interruption and overlaps in English learners' L2 French talk, while Huth (2006) examines English learners' sequence organization during compliment response in L2 German. Shively (2015) analyzes English learners' listener responses in L2 Spanish conversations. Preference structure is often examined in requests among learners across different proficiency levels – for example, in L2 Arabic (Al-Gahtani and Roever, 2014), L2 German (Taleghani-Nikazm and Huth, 2010), and L2 Chinese (Su and Ren, 2017).

2.1.6 Prosody

Prosodic features may influence pragmatic meaning. However, despite the importance of prosody in conveying meaning, it has been neglected in L2 pragmatics (see Kang and Kermad, 2019 for an overview). This lack of research on prosody in L2 pragmatic production may be due to "the lack of a systematic analytical methodology" (Romero-Trillo, 2019: 91). Therefore, Romero-Trillo (2019) proposes an approach to explore the prosodic aspects of pragmatic markers as feedback produced by native and non-native speakers in corpus pragmatics.

Verdugo and Romero-Trillo (2005) carried out one of the few studies that compares the intonation in reading tag questions between Spanish learners of English and native speakers of English. The results revealed that the learners and the native speakers used a similar rising intonation pattern in questioning tags, but, in confirmation tags, while the native speakers used an unmarked tone to indicate certainty and demand agreement, the learners again used a rising intonation. The authors concluded that a lack of pragmatic knowledge and awareness of the functions of tag questions led to the Spanish learners' overuse of a rising intonation.

2.1.7 Concluding Remarks

In summary, pragmatic production studies have investigated a variety of pragmatic features, although with different degrees of attention. However, the studies predominantly examine learners at university level. An underdeveloped area concerns investigation of learners of different ages. Rose (2000) investigated pragmatic development of requests, apologies, and compliment responses among three groups of primary school EFL (English as a Foreign Language) learners in Hong Kong (aged approximately 7, 9, and 11). Barón Parés (2012) examined request development in Catalan-Spanish bilingual EFL learners aged 10, 12, 16, and 18–19. Savić *et al.* (2021) investigated the request production of young EFL learners in Greek Cypriot and Norwegian aged 9, 11, and 13. More acquisition studies are needed to explore the pragmatic development of learners across different ages.

More importantly, pragmatic production studies tend to focus on nuanced data coding but lack a solid theoretical orientation. It is often documented that learners may underuse or overuse certain pragmatic features compared with native speakers. However, studies should also explore why such divergence exists by investigating a multiplicity of factors simultaneously, particularly concerning the pragmatic norms of L1 and L2, learners' L2 proficiency, and pragmatic agency.

2.2 Pragmatic Perception

Studies on learner pragmatic perception can be roughly divided into two categories, namely pragmatic awareness and pragmatic comprehension, which will be reviewed in the following two subsections respectively.

2.2.1 Pragmatic Awareness

Pragmatic awareness refers to learners' conscious knowledge or evaluation of certain pragmatic features or practice. This line of research mainly investigates learners' ability to detect pragmatically (in)appropriate language uses and reflexivity on pragmatic phenomena. The following sections will introduce the key themes investigated in the pragmatic awareness literature.

Appropriateness of Speech Acts

Bardovi-Harlig and Dörnyei (1998) pioneered investigation into the relationship between pragmatic awareness and grammatical awareness. They focused on awareness in the sense of noticing in Schmidt's noticing hypothesis (1993, 2001), which refers to "registering the simple occurrence of some event" (Schmidt, 1993: 26). They compared EFL learners in Hungary with ESL (English as a Second Language) learners in the United States using a video-prompted task they developed, which included refusals, apologies, requests, and suggestions. The task required participants to distinguish grammatical errors and pragmatic infelicitous items, and to rate both for severity. The findings indicated that both learning contexts and L2 proficiency influenced the learners' performance, and study-abroad length also played an important role in developing learner pragmatic awareness.

Bardovi-Harlig and Dörnyei's seminal work was replicated in many different contexts, sometimes yielding different results. Also using the video-prompted task, Schauer (2009) investigated German learners' pragmatic awareness and found that the learners increased their pragmatic awareness significantly during study abroad in the UK. In contrast, Niezgoda and Roever (2001) compared EFL learners in the Czech Republic with ESL learners at a US language school; using the same video-prompted instrument, they found that overall the EFL learners outperformed the ESL learners at error identification and severity rating for both grammatical and pragmatic items. Study-abroad length had a clear effect on learners' pragmatic awareness, but L2 proficiency did not have an impact. Surprisingly, however, the longer the learners stayed in the target community, the more tolerant they were to pragmatic infelicities.

Some studies adapted the video-prompted task developed by Bardovi-Harlig and Dörnyei (1998) into questionnaires. For example, Xu *et al.* (2009) used a paper-and-pencil version of the conversations and investigated learners with a mix of L1s living in the United States with different study-abroad lengths and L2 proficiency levels. Ren (2015) compared the development of pragmatic awareness among EFL learners and ESL learners, only focusing on pragmatic items. Ren did not ask the learners to detect whether an item was infelicitous; instead, he asked the learners to directly evaluate the appropriateness of the item. Some researchers translated the questionnaire into other languages to explore learner pragmatic awareness in different target languages; Rodriguez (2001) used the questionnaire in Spanish to investigate the effect of study abroad in Spain on learners' awareness of request strategies. The participants were asked to decide whether utterances were appropriate, and if not, to rate how inappropriate they were using a four-point scale with no neutral point. Bella (2012a) adapted the questionnaire to investigate the effect of residence length in Greece on learners' pragmatic awareness in L2 Greek.

Several researchers have modified Bardovi-Harlig and Dörnyei's (1998) methodology in order to fit their own investigations. For example, Yang (2019) developed fourteen scenarios for expressing gratitude and examined the effect of proficiency on L2 Chinese learners' pragmatic and grammatical awareness. Bardovi-Harlig and Griffin (2005) went a step further by requiring learners not only to detect the inappropriateness in roleplays but also to repair it. Yang and Ren (2019) used the pragmatic awareness questionnaire to explore the relationship between pragmatic awareness and Chinese EFL learners' motivation to learn English, while Lv *et al.* (2021) translated the questionnaire into Chinese and explored the relationship between willingness to communicate and pragmatic awareness among L2 learners of Chinese with a mix of L1s.

Researchers have also designed other methods to explore learners' pragmatic awareness. Takahashi (2005) investigated whether the pragmatic awareness of Japanese EFL learners was related to their learning motivation and language proficiency. Learners' awareness of the target pragmalinguistic features, including three forms of request head acts, discourse markers, idiomatic expressions, and non-idiomatic expressions, was assessed using a seven-point Likert scale questionnaire. The findings indicated that the learners' pragmatic awareness correlated with their intrinsic motivation but not with their L2 proficiency. Economidou-Kogetsidis (2016) investigated differences in the evaluations of the (im)politeness of student email requests and the personality of the sender between English lecturers and Greek-Cypriot L2 university students. The learners were found to be unaware of the negative consequences of an inappropriate academic email, as they seemed to equate politeness with formality. The author pointed out that the learners viewed the student–faculty emails as purely transactional, while the English lecturers viewed them as both transactional and interactional.

Conventional Expressions

A number of perception studies have explored learners' pragmatic awareness of conventional expressions. Bardovi-Harlig (2009) examined the production and recognition of conventional expressions among English learners with mixed L1s through an oral production task and an aural recognition task. Recognition was detected by a three-level familiarity estimate in the form "I often/sometimes/never hear this". The results showed that recognition of conventional expressions was a necessary but not sufficient condition for production.

Using the same dataset, Bardovi-Harlig and Bastos (2011) investigated the effects of proficiency, length of study abroad, and intensity of interaction on L2 English learners' recognition and production of conventional expressions. Only intensity of interaction was found to have a significant influence on the recognition of conventional expressions. However, it is worth noting that the majority of the learners in Bardovi-Harlig and Bastos (2011) had studied abroad in the United States for less than eight months. The relatively narrow range of study-abroad length may have limited the benefit of study abroad (Taguchi and Li, 2019).

Based on her earlier work (Bardovi-Harlig, 2009), Bardovi-Harlig (2014) investigated L2 learners' awareness of the meaning of conventional expressions in English using an aural Vocabulary Knowledge Scale questionnaire. It was found that the learners' awareness of the meaning of the conventional expressions influenced their uses of such expressions. In addition, it was likely that the learners acquired the form of a conventional expression first, gradually grasping its plausible meaning and refining it rather than acquiring the form and correct meaning at the same time. Alcón Soler and Sánchez-Hernández (2017) compared the development of learners' production and recognition of conventional expressions during study abroad. They found that the ability to recognize the conventional expressions seemed to be a first step for the latter acquisition of the productive ability, echoing the findings in Bardovi-Harlig (2014). Also using a Vocabulary Knowledge Scale questionnaire, Sánchez-Hernández and Alcón Soler (2019) explored the development of Brazilian learners of English in terms of their recognition of pragmatic routines during study abroad, and examined how sociocultural adaptation and intensity of interaction influenced their development. The findings revealed that the learners' recognition of pragmatic routines significantly improved after a semester study abroad, influenced by both sociocultural adaptation and intensity of interaction. L2 exposure and learners' willingness to socialize in the target environment were determinant factors in recognizing pragmatic routines.

A couple of studies have investigated learners' pragmatic awareness of conventional expressions in L2 French. Kinginger and Blattner (2008) reported on three L2 French learners' awareness of colloquial phrases during a study-abroad semester in France. In a language awareness interview, participants were asked to comment on their knowledge of the use of French colloquial phrases.

The findings suggested that the learners developed their awareness of socio-pragmatic variability during study abroad, and their performance was related to their identity and their participation in French-speaking contexts. Edmonds (2014) investigated the effect of study-abroad length in France on L2 French learners' evaluation of naturalness of conventional expressions across a long-stay group (over a year) and a short-stay group (four to six months). The results showed that as with native speakers, the two groups of learners judged the conventional expressions similarly and significantly different from grammatical but not from conventional strings. However, native speakers could detect conventional expressions more quickly than nonconventional expressions, but the learners' reaction times for the two types were not significantly different.

Address Terms

Similar to production studies, research on learners' pragmatic awareness of address terms has tended to investigate languages other than English. Kinginger and Farrell (2004) focused on the development of eight American French learners' sociopragmatic awareness of French address terms (*tu* vs. *vous*) using language awareness interviews, biweekly journals, and observer field notes. In the interviews the learners were presented with a series of six social situations illustrating different parameters influencing address term use, for example, set-ting, age, and familiarity of interlocutor, and were asked to choose an address term for each of the situations and explain the rationales underlying their choices. The findings showed that the learners developed their awareness of French address terms but the development did not relate to their linguistic competence.

Villarreal (2014) investigated pragmatic production and awareness of Spanish address forms (*tú* vs. *usted*) among English learners of Spanish. Data were collected using roleplays and metapragmatic judgment questionnaires. Analysis of the judgment questionnaire revealed that the learners were aware of the indexical function of the second person address forms, although some learners failed to consistently produce their desired address forms. Finally, Blood (2018) examined the pragmatic awareness of Australian learners of German with respect to the second-person pronoun *du* during a six-week language course in Germany. The findings revealed that even a short length of study abroad, such as six weeks in this study, could facilitate improvement in learners' pragmatic awareness of address terms.

2.2.2 Pragmatic Comprehension

Research on pragmatic comprehension investigates learners' abilities to under-stand the implied meaning of an utterance, which may be different to what is said. Studies in this area generally employ multiple-choice questionnaires to examine learners' understanding of a range of pragmatic aspects.

Comprehension of Conversation Implicature

Studies frequently compare learners' abilities to infer different types of conversation implicature. Bouton (1994) was one of the first to investigate the effect of study-abroad length on learners' comprehension of implicatures, showing that learners became more proficient in their interpretation of implicatures to a statistically significant degree. Nevertheless, even after seventeen months of study-abroad experience, the learners still had difficulties in comprehending understated criticism, sequence implicatures, and Pope Q implicature (this type of implicature answers one question with another highly formulaic question, for example, "Is the Pope Catholic?"), which did not consistently cause trouble for learners with over 4.5 years of study-abroad experience. Cook and Liddicoat (2002) investigated the effect of proficiency on L2 English learners' comprehension of request strategies, revealing significant differences in the comprehension accuracy of request types between two learner groups (low vs. high proficiency), with the high proficiency learners providing a significantly higher number of interpretations of conventional and nonconventional indirect requests than the low proficiency learners.

A series of studies were conducted to investigate learner comprehension of indirect meaning. For example, Taguchi (2005) investigated the effect of proficiency on L2 learners' comprehension of indirect utterances in dialogues in terms of accuracy and speed of comprehension. Participants were asked to complete a computerized listening task consisting of two types of conversation implicatures that were different in terms of their conventionality (conventionally indirect request or refusal vs. idiosyncratic implicature). The results revealed that the learners processed the more conventional utterances more quickly and more accurately than the less conventional utterances. In contrast, native speakers could process the two types almost equally in terms of accuracy and speed. These findings suggested a significant effect of L2 proficiency on learners' comprehension accuracy but not on comprehension speed for both types of implied meaning. Taguchi (2008b, 2009a) also found a proficiency effect on comprehension accuracy but not on speed in L2 Japanese learners' comprehension of indirect refusals and indirect opinions (conventional vs. nonconventional). Both studies found that refusals were the easiest to comprehend, followed by conventional and nonconventional indirect opinions.

Taguchi also examined the development of the comprehension of implied refusals and opinions among Japanese EFL (2007a) and ESL (2008a) learners at beginner level. The results showed that the Japanese EFL learners' comprehension accuracy and speed improved significantly over seven weeks, although comprehension speed increased much less compared to the accuracy of comprehension (Taguchi, 2007a). The Japanese ESL learners made significant progress in terms of comprehension speed, but showed little improvement in comprehension accuracy over four months (Taguchi, 2008a). The development of comprehension accuracy did not correlate with the amount of language contact for any skills (speaking, listening, reading, writing), whereas the development of comprehension speed correlated significantly with the amount of speaking and reading.

To further explore the effect of learning environment on learners' pragmatic comprehension of indirect refusals and indirect opinions, Taguchi (2008c) compared Japanese EFL and ESL learners at the beginner level over seven weeks. The results showed that both groups' comprehension accuracy and speed improved significantly over time, suggesting that pragmatic comprehension developed over time regardless of the learning environment. Comparisons of effect sizes revealed that for the EFL group, the magnitude of effect was much less for speed than for accuracy, whereas the ESL group showed a significant improvement in speed but only marginal improvement in accuracy. The EFL group showed a significantly greater improvement compared to the ESL group in the comprehension accuracy of indirect refusals but not of indirect opinions, indicating that "different environments may support different aspects of pragmatic comprehension ability" (Taguchi, 2008c: 444). In another study adopting a similar design, Taguchi (2011a) examined the effect of proficiency and study-abroad experience on Japanese English learners' pragmatic comprehension of indirect refusals and routines. The results of this study indicated a significant effect of proficiency, but no effect of study-abroad experience, on the learners' comprehension speed. Both proficiency and study-abroad experience had significant effects on the learners' comprehension accuracy, but separate analyses of indirect refusals and routines revealed a significant effect of study abroad on the learners' comprehension accuracy of routines but not indirect refusals.

Köylü (2018) moved a step further by asking learners to orally report their inferences of conversational implicatures in English in an audio-visual interpretation task. The results showed that the learners' comprehension of conversational implicatures had a positive correlation with their L2 proficiency. Chen and Lin (2021) used multiple-choice DCTs to compare Chinese EFL learners' comprehension of conversational implicatures between individual and collaborative work. They found that the individual and collaborative learners performed similarly.

A couple of studies have explored learners' abilities to determine the illocutionary force of indirect speech acts. Garcia (2004) examined L2 learners across low and high proficiency levels in terms of their comprehension of nonconventional indirect speech acts and detection of the illocutionary force of an utterance, using a four-option multiple-choice task: requesting, offering, suggesting, and correcting. The results showed that the high proficiency learners were more successful than the low proficiency learners, reflecting a positive effect of proficiency on speech act recognition. Linguistic features such as explicit agents and modal use helped the learners to detect the illocutionary force of a nonconventional indirect speech act. Meanwhile Holtgraves (2007) pursued this issue from a different angle, exploring whether learners could automatically recognize the illocutionary force when they read indirect speech act utterances. Participants were asked to read conversational utterances and perform a lexical decision task to determine whether a target string of letters on a screen was a word. It was found that native speakers performed the task more quickly when the string was the speech act associated with the preceding utterance, but learners did not show any difference, suggesting that they could not yet activate automatic comprehension of speech acts.

Although the above studies all explored conversation implicatures in English, some studies focused on L2 Spanish to examine learners' comprehension of implicature. For example, Koike (1996) investigated whether learners of Spanish across various proficiency levels could understand the speech act of suggestion. Learners were asked to identify the types of speech act expressed in seven video-taped situations, to reproduce the speech acts, and to evaluate the speakers in terms of five aspects: aggressive vs. passive, rude vs. polite, noncommunicative vs. communicative, strong vs. weak, and unfriendly vs. friendly. It was found that two lower-proficiency groups had difficulties in comprehending the intent of the speech acts whereas more advanced learners succeeded in recognizing the suggestions, indicating a clear proficiency effect. Taguchi *et al.* (2016a) explored L2 Spanish learners' comprehension of three types of indirect meaning, indirect refusals, indirect opinions, and irony, in terms of comprehension accuracy and speed. The results showed that the learners comprehended indirect refusals and opinions the same in terms of their accuracy, but they comprehended indirect opinions much faster than indirect refusals and irony, suggesting that conventionality did not facilitate the learners' pragmatic comprehension. Irony was found to be the most difficult to comprehend among the three types for the L2 Spanish learners; this may be due to the difficulty of comprehending irony in a second language.

Comprehension of Scalar Implicature

Scalar implicature is a particular type of implicature in which an additional meaning is inferred with respect to a gradable scale, for example <some, all>. Slabakova (2010) examined how Korean English learners processed the quantifiers *some* and *all* in sentences with and without contexts, with results showing that the learners had no difficulties in interpreting the scalar implicatures. Snape and Hosoi (2018) investigated the influence of L2 proficiency on learners' understanding of the scalar implicatures *some* and *all* by examining intermediate and advanced Japanese English learners. This study found no significant differences between either the native speakers and the learners or the two learner groups, indicating that L2 proficiency did not have an effect on the learners' acquisition of scalar implicatures.

Using oral rather than written stimuli, Mazzaggio *et al.* (2021) tested Italian university students' understanding of the scalar implicatures *some* and *all* in English and their equivalents in Italian and Spanish. All the learners were tested using utterances spoken in either their L1 Italian or an L2 (English or Spanish). The results showed that learners were less likely to derive an underinformative interpretation in L2 than in L1 condition, suggesting that deriving such pragmatic interpretations was costly and nonautomatic in an L2.

Unlike English, Spanish has two indefinite determiners, *unos* and *algunos*, which have nearly identical meanings (close to *some* in English) but differ in terms of their felicitousness in different contexts (Miller *et al.*, 2016). Comparing English learners of Spanish at a near-native level with Spanish native speakers, Miller *et al.* (2016) found that the advanced English learners were able to achieve native-like judgment of the two Spanish scalar terms.

Comprehension of Irony

Only a few studies have focused on L2 pragmatic comprehension of irony. Kim (2014) examined how Korean professionals understood sarcasm in spoken English in five video clips of the sitcom *Friends*. Participants were asked to complete three tasks: identify the instance of sarcasm, interpret the speaker intention and the communicative goal, and report the cues and their thoughts during their detection and comprehension. The majority of the Korean participants reported that they had to use a significant amount of guesswork to complete the tasks, suggesting the difficulty of understanding sarcasm in L2. In addition, the results also revealed that the Korean learners identified English sarcastic utterances and interpreted speaker intention by drawing on their L1 pragmalinguistic and general linguistic knowledge.

Ellis *et al.* (2021) investigated Chinese university students' ability to identify irony in English using an irony test. The results showed that the Chinese learners' scores were much lower than those of native speakers. The learners performed better in identifying negative irony than positive irony, and both L2 proficiency and study-abroad length showed statistically significant relationships with irony recognition, although these relationships were found to be weak.

Comprehension of Humor

Besides irony, humor is also believed to be difficult to grasp in L2. Chen and Dewaele (2019) asked Chinese learners of English to rate the funniness and the ease of understanding of two short video extracts containing humorous utterances. The findings showed that there was a significant difference between the Chinese learners and the English native speakers in terms of their funniness and ease of understanding ratings. It was revealed that proficiency and funniness ratings were unrelated at the lower and upper intermediate levels, but related at the advanced level.

Bell *et al.* (2021) developed a paper-and-pencil version of a DCT to solicit learners' responses to ten scenarios encouraging them to respond with humor. The learners were asked to fill in the DCT and evaluate whether they felt their responses were funny. The results showed that humor target (self vs. other) as well as learners' L1 and L2 affected their perceptions of humor.

Comprehension of Contextual Cues

Nonlinguistic features such as contextual cues can also influence speakers' utterance meanings. Nakamura *et al.* (2020) investigated whether there was an integrative function of contrastive pitch accent and visual contextual cues in assisting the processing of referential ambiguous syntactic structure for English native speakers and Japanese L2 English learners. This study found that a visually presented context was helpful for both the native speakers and the learners in comprehending ambiguous utterances. Prosodic cues helped the native speakers to resolve referential ambiguity with visual cues present, but the learners were unable to integrate prosody with reference to visual cues. Cho and Dewaele (2021) investigated Korean learners' pragmatic difficulties when perceiving English emotional intonation. In this study, the learners were required to rate the valence (positive vs. negative) and intensity (weak vs. strong) of emotional sentences on a nine-point scale. The results indicated that the Korean learners had difficulties in perceiving intentional meanings through pitch as a prosodic cue in English interactions.

Ishida (2006) investigated L2 Japanese learners' receptive knowledge of contextual cues. Data were collected using stimulated recall, a multiple-choice task, and a five-point rating scale for the importance of the cues. The findings revealed differences between the Japanese native speakers and the L2 Japanese learners in terms of their perception and interpretation of the contextual cues.

2.2.3 Concluding Remarks

Evaluation of the (in)appropriateness of language uses is one of the often-examined issues in pragmatic awareness research. This topic was pioneered by Bardovi-Harlig and Dörnyei (1998) to examine learners' ability to detect pragmatically (in)felicitous speech acts, tapping both pragmalinguistic and sociopragmatic knowledge. The methodology was developed more than two decades ago and has been replicated and adapted in many contexts. More innovative designs are needed to further explore this issue. In addition, learners' reflexivity on conventional expressions has also been investigated, which is examined in terms of familiarity or meanings of such expressions. That is, pragmatic awareness research on conventional expressions focuses more on pragmalinguistic knowledge, while sociopragmatic knowledge is barely touched upon.

Pragmatic comprehension research has covered a range of topics, including conversation implicature, scalar implicature, irony, humor and contextual cues such as pitch and intonation. However, the research would increase its rigour if it were conducted under the theoretical frameworks in pragmatics. For example, the studies divided conventionality of conversation implicature differently from Grice's (1989) framework on implicature. Future research may want to follow the classification of Grice (1989) to link better L2 pragmatic comprehension literature to general pragmatics. In addition, pragmatic comprehension research is often conducted in a lab setting. Future studies should investigate learners' pragmatic comprehension in authentic communication. This applies to pragmatic awareness research as well.

2.3 Research Modality

Second language pragmatics learning has predominantly investigated learners' pragmatic competence in face-to-face oral communication, although many studies collect data using written-for-oral tasks (Bardovi-Harlig, 2018) – for example, using written DCTs to explore oral pragmatic competence. Only a couple of studies have examined learners' written pragmatic competence; Youn (2014) investigated the relationships among learners' L2 pragmatics in writing tasks, syntactic complexity, and L2 proficiency. Syntactic complexity was analyzed in three aspects: mean length of T-unit, mean length of clause, and mean number of clauses per T-unit. The results showed that the three measures of syntactic complexity were not strongly related to increases in L2 proficiency and pragmatic competence. Comparatively, the increases in mean length of T-unit were more related to different levels of proficiency and pragmatics than the other two measures. Similarly, Chen (2020) analyzed Chinese EFL writers' use of single-author in academic writing, while Taguchi *et al.* (2021) examined Chinese EFL learners' advice-giving in written texts.

The fact that learners' writing pragmatic competence is under-researched may be due in part to two reasons. On the one hand, pragmatists, including L2 pragmatists, still value oral communication over written texts. Thus, except for historical pragmatics, pragmatics research prefers oral communication over written. On the other hand, many scholars investigate L2 learners' writing such as formulaic expressions (e.g., Pérez-Llantada, 2014) and meta-discourse (e.g., Hyland, 2019; Qin and Uccelli, 2019), but they conduct research under the perspectives of L2 writing and academic discourse rather than L2 pragmatics.

Compared with written communication, L2 pragmatics has paid more attention to learners' pragmatic competence in internet-mediated communication. This stream of work can be traced at least to the beginning of this century; for example, Belz and Kinginger (2002) showcased the learning and use of informal vs. formal T-/V-form second person pronouns by two American students, one studying French and one studying German, in web-based contact including email and synchronous chat with their key pals in France and Germany, respectively.

However, most of the L2 pragmatics studies on internet-mediated communication have been conducted in this decade. Email is a frequently explored communicative genre (e.g., Chen *et al.*, 2016; Economidou-Kogetsidis *et al.*, 2021), in both pragmatic production (e.g., Barón and Ortega, 2018; Economidou-Kogetsidis, 2018; Savić and Đorđević, 2021) and perception (e.g., Economidou-Kogetsidis, 2016; Ren and Liu, 2021; Winans, 2020). Researchers often employ electronic DCTs (EDCTs) to investigate email literacy, and this is more legitimate than using written DCTs for exploring oral communication; although email is a hybrid of oral and written, it is essentially more like a written genre.

Researchers have also investigated learners' pragmatic competence in various types of internet-mediated communication, including digital stories (García-Pastor, 2020), web conferences (Cunningham, 2017), gameplay (Tang and Taguchi, 2021), and social media such as Facebook (Blattner and Fiori, 2012), Reddit (Yeh and Swinehart, 2020), Skype (Barron and Black, 2015), and WhatsApp (García-Gómez, 2020). Most research has documented the benefit of internet-mediated communication in helping learners to develop their L2 pragmatic competence. However, García-Gómez (2020) found that without careful design or training, social media platforms such as WhatsApp may also be detrimental for learners' L2 pragmatic development because they may encounter more cases of misunderstanding on WhatsApp.

As the above reviews show, L2 pragmatics learning has investigated oral, written, and internet-mediated communication. It is vital for researchers to "converge on modality" (Bardovi-Harlig, 2018: 16) in L2 pragmatics research. That is, if researchers wish to investigate learners' pragmatic competence in oral communication, it must be investigated by oral tasks; in written communication, it must be investigated by written tasks; and in internet-mediated communication, it must be investigated in the context of online platforms. However, there were some studies that used written tasks to measure learners' oral production, which posed a serious threat to the validity of the findings (see Section 4.2 for more discussion on validity).

2.4 Summary

This section reviewed studies investigating learners' acquisition in pragmatic production and perception. Some studies on conventional expressions examined both facets. In contrast, learners' production and perception were often analyzed separately in other pragmatic features. Future studies are encouraged to investigate the two facets of pragmatic competence in the same groups of learners to explore the relation between productive and receptive pragmatic competences. In addition, except for studies on perception of contextual cues, the research only examines the linguistic resource in pragmatic competence. The semiotic and multimodal resources have not attracted attention, even in the internet-mediated communication where such resources are used pervasively.

Furthermore, although increasingly researchers have investigated learners' pragmatic learning, there are still a large number of studies only examining learners' pragmatic use. They investigate learners' pragmatic performance at the time of data collection, and thus they can be classified as single-moment studies (Kasper and Rose, 1999). The focus on pragmatic use rather than learning is a partially cause of the peripheral position of L2 pragmatics in general L2 research (Ren, 2015). Future studies should stop treating learners as a homogenous group and simply comparing their pragmatic performance with that of native speakers. It is more insightful to investigate the pattern of learners' pragmatic development and the association between pragmatic learning and linguistic learning (i.e., vocabulary, grammar) for uncovering the underlying mechanisms of pragmatic learning and suggesting useful implications for pragmatic instruction. The next section reviews the role of pragmatic teaching.

3 Second Language Pragmatics Teaching

This section introduces research on L2 pragmatics instruction, which is much less common than work on L2 pragmatics learning. Research in this field has mainly focused on two questions: 1) Is teaching effective in L2 pragmatics? and 2) Which approach is more effective in teaching L2 pragmatics? We will analyze these two questions respectively in the following subsections.

3.1 Effects of Teaching Second Language Pragmatics

Literature on L2 pragmatics learning has documented that mere exposure is not sufficient for pragmatic development in an L2, even after a long stay in the target language community (e.g., Barron, 2003; Ren, 2019b; Schauer, 2009), because "pragmatic functions and relevant contextual factors are often not salient to learners and so not likely to be noticed despite prolonged exposure" (Kasper and Rose, 2002: 237). Therefore, much of the literature on pragmatics learning calls for pragmatics intervention to assist learners to develop their L2 pragmatic competence (e.g., Ren, 2013; Taguchi, 2015b), which is generally neglected in L2 classrooms or textbooks (Ren and Han, 2016).

Early studies on L2 pragmatics teaching were stimulated by Kasper's (1997) seminal talk, "Can Pragmatic competence be taught?". After summarizing a dozen prior studies on teaching pragmatics, Kasper's answer to this question was affirmative. The next few years saw increasing numbers of empirical studies on L2 pragmatics teaching (see Section 3.2) and synthetic works, including narrative reviews (Kasper and Rose, 1999; Rose, 2005; Taguchi, 2011c), syntheses (Taguchi, 2015b; Takahashi, 2010), and meta-analyses (Badjadi, 2016; Jeon and Kaya, 2006; Plonsky and Zhuang, 2019; Yousefi and Nassaji, 2019), all of which showed that pragmatics is teachable and pragmatic instruction can facilitate learners' L2 pragmatic development. It is fair to say that L2 pragmatics scholars have reached a consensus regarding the question of whether teaching is effective in pragmatics; therefore, readers who are interested in L2 pragmatics instruction should shift their attention from exploring whether teaching is helpful in pragmatics to how to teach pragmatics effectively. This is the topic of the next section.

3.2 Approaches in Second Language Pragmatics Teaching

To date, the most investigated teaching approaches in L2 pragmatics have been explicit and implicit teaching. Researchers adopt definitions given by Kasper (2001), in which explicit teaching involves metapragmatic explanations of pragmalinguistic uses and/or sociopragmatic rules of target pragmatic features, while implicit teaching does not include such metapragmatic explanation but rather employs various methods to facilitate learners' unconscious reflection on pragmatic uses of target pragmatic features by themselves.

Implicit teaching consists of a range of different approaches, of which some focus on input, some on output, and others on interaction in completing tasks. This section starts with studies on interventions in terms of input enhancement, which refers to the manipulation of input to make specific target features more salient to learners (Sharwood-Smith, 1993), either phonologically or typographically. In L2 pragmatics teaching, input enhancement is manipulated through various forms such as input flood, textual enhancement, and consciousness raising, which are at different positions along the implicit–explicit continuum. As many studies combine different teaching approaches in various ways, it may be more beneficial to investigate the instructional methods separately. Therefore, I will begin with the most implicit tactic and move on to consider the less implicit ones. If two teaching interventions are combined, I will review them in terms of the less implicit teaching method.

3.2.1 Input Flood

Input flood is a pedagogical technique that attempts to make specific pragmatic features more frequent in input without doing anything else to draw the learner's attention to the features (Wong, 2005). The input may be written or aural. The expectation is that the artificial increase in the frequency of the pragmatic feature will aid the learner in noticing it.

Not many studies have employed input flood in teaching pragmatics. However, a couple of studies have reported its effectiveness. Hernández (2011) examined the effects of input flood with and without explicit instruction on learners' use of Spanish discourse makers to narrate an event in the past time frame. Both groups were provided with the opportunity for communicative practice, although only the group that was exposed to explicit teaching received feedback as well. The results suggested that input flood had a positive impact on both learner groups' use of discourse markers. Fordyce (2014) investigated the effect of input flood and explicit teaching on learners' uses of epistemic stance in writing, showing the effectiveness of an input flood intervention even if it did not deliberately encourage learners to notice the target forms. Fakher Ajabshir (2022) investigated the effects of input flood, textual enhancement, and output-based instruction on Iranian EFL learners' comprehension and production of external and internal modification of requests. The findings revealed the effectiveness of input flood in teaching the request modification. However, examining adolescent German L2 English learners' use of pragmatic markers, Haselow

(2021) reported that input flood with communication practice did not improve the frequency and range of the learners' use of the markers.

Studies disagree more on the comparative effects of input flood when combined with other teaching techniques. Hernández (2011) reported that although learners receiving a combination of explicit teaching and input flood used slightly more discourse markers than learners with input flood alone, the two methods did not lead to a significant difference in developing the learners' use of Spanish discourse markers. In contrast, employing a similar design to Hernández (2011) involving a comparison of input flood with and without explicit instruction, Haselow (2021) found that only explicit teaching led to German English learners' improvement in the use of pragmatic markers. Fakher Ajabshir (2022) also concluded that input flood yielded the smallest effect on learners' improvement with respect to the comprehension and production of external and internal modification of requests, compared with textual enhancement and output-based instruction.

Although we cannot draw conclusions based on these studies, it is fair to say that different pragmatic markers and external vs. internal request modification may be different in terms of their salience and processing difficulty, which may affect the relative effects of input flood. In addition, the potential influences of the number of pragmatic features in input flood and the length of the teaching cannot be excluded.

3.2.2 Textual Enhancement

Textual enhancement makes certain pragmatic features more salient in the input through different forms, such as boldface, underline, and color coding for special stress in written input, and intonation in spoken input. For example, Alcón Soler (2005) investigated the effect of instruction on Spanish high school EFL learners' awareness and production of requests, putting request strategies in bold on the scripts and putting sociopragmatic factors involved in requesting in capital letters and bold. The results showed that both learners' awareness and production of requests improved after the instruction.

Some studies combine input from different modalities to strengthen the potential effects. Fukuya and Martínez-Flor (2008) investigated the interactive effects of teaching approach (explicit and implicit) and assessment tasks (email and phone) on Spanish EFL learners' use of suggestion strategies and hedges. The implicit group received enhanced input by watching videotaped situations with captions of targeted suggestions in boldface and the social factors involved in each situation. The results showed that the explicit group made significantly more improvement than the implicit group in the phone task, but the improvement of the two groups was similar in the email task. Likewise, in Fakher Ajabshir (2022) a textual enhancement group watched short video dialogues depicting request acts that included captions with the target feature bold and underlined. After watching the video clips they were also provided with a handout including transcripts of the dialogues with the target features highlighted. The results indicated an effect of textual enhancement on learners' production and comprehension of request modification.

3.2.3 Consciousness-raising

Consciousness-raising implies that the learner's mental state is altered by the activity (Sharwood-Smith, 1993). It is positioned at the more explicit end of the implicit–explicit continuum and is more frequently investigated in L2 pragmatics than input flood and textual enhancement.

Many studies have demonstrated the benefits of consciousness-raising activities on learners' pragmatic development. Takimoto (2008, 2009) compared the effects of three teaching approaches on Japanese EFL learners' production and awareness of request strategies: consciousness-raising tasks including comparing and identifying forms of requests, and structured input tasks asking students to consciously notice the use of a request with, and without, explicit information. The results showed that all the teaching groups performed significantly better than the control group, who performed equally well on request production tested by DCTs and roleplays and on pragmatic appropriateness judgment tasks measured by listening tests and acceptability judgments. Takimoto (2012) investigated the effects of consciousness-raising tasks with and without meta-pragmatic discussion on Japanese learners' recognition and production of English request downgraders, finding that the two groups made improvements in their recognition and production of request downgraders. In terms of recognition, the two teaching conditions did not differ in terms of improvements in the students' performance, indicating that regardless of metapragmatic discussion, consciousness-raising tasks can enhance learners' pragmatic recognition of request downgraders. In terms of production, it was found that the group receiving metapragmatic discussion improved more than the group without such discussion.

Researchers have also examined this teaching technique in languages other than English. Narita (2012) investigated the effects of consciousness-raising teaching on L2 Japanese learners' acquisition of evidential markers such as '*rashii* (I heard that)'. The learners were given training in comparing target features in English and Japanese on the one hand, and learners' and Japanese native speakers' uses on the other hand. The findings showed the learners' development in both their production and metapragmatic awareness of the target evidential markers.

Alsuhaibani (2020) compared the effects of consciousness-raising and corpus-based instruction on EFL learners' compliment responses. The consciousness-raising activities included comparing types and frequencies of compliment responses in L1 and L2, collecting L2 compliment responses from the media, comparing felicitous and infelicitous uses of compliment responses, and roleplays. The corpus group searched the Corpus of Contemporary American English (COCA) to retrieve authentic compliment responses and compared L1 and L2 compliment responses using the corpus. The results showed the effectiveness of both teaching interventions to the learners in terms of their compliment responses, which did not yield significant differences between the two approaches. This finding is feasible because both approaches raised the learners' awareness and helped them to notice the use of the target pragmatic features.

The effects of consciousness-raising on the acquisition of conventional expressions have also been examined. Bardovi-Harlig and Vellenga (2012) investigated the effect of activities designed to help learners to notice the function of target expressions on recognition and the use of conventional expressions. The results showed that the presentation of contextualized examples with guided noticing activities seemed to promote the learners' use and recognition of conventional expressions that were relatively transparent and consistent with their grammatical competence.

Furniss (2016) examined the effect of a corpus-assisted website on L1 English learners' aural recognition and comprehension of Russian routine formulas. The website was designed to help learners to notice the functions of routine formulas in authentic situations, including activating background knowledge of target routines, translation activities, description of the formula's functions with examples, cloze activities, dialogue turn matching, and free and integrated production practice. The results indicated that the instruction improved the learners' awareness of the target routine formulas and helped them detect nonsensical phrases.

Recast is generally defined as a reformulation of non-target-like utterances into more target-like forms while preserving the original meaning (Long, 1996), which is in essence a form of consciousness-raising. Many studies combine textual enhancement with recast; for example, Alcón Soler (2007) investigated the effect of textual enhancement and recast during roleplays on learners' awareness of suggestions. The results revealed that the combination of the two implicit teaching techniques was as effective as explicit teaching in improving learners' pragmatic awareness. Similarly, Nguyen *et al.* (2017) examined the effects of visual textual enhancement in the format of bolded target structures combined with recasts on Vietnamese EFL learners' performance of criticism between peers. The learners were tested by three production tasks, including DCT, roleplay, and oral peer-feedback task. The results indicated that the learners improved their pragmatic performance in terms of appropriateness, accuracy, and external and internal modifiers of criticism. Ahmadian (2020) examined the effect of textual enhancement and teachers' recast in learners' roleplays on their production of refusals and judgment of the appropriateness of refusals in conversations. Only one recast per performance and two for each pair of learners were provided. The results revealed that the teaching enhanced the learners' production and pragmatic awareness of refusals. In addition, the learners' working memory capacity scores were positively and strongly correlated with their gains.

3.2.4 Output-based Teaching

The output-based teaching approach is built on the Output Hypothesis proposed by Swain (1985), who argues that production (i.e., output) really forces learners to undertake syntactic processing and enhances the L2 development most effectively. Output in second language acquisition (SLA) is not whatever learners produce; it is the language that learners produce to express meanings (VanPatten, 2003). This approach emphasizes the critical role for opportunities in which learners are "pushed" to produce improved or modified output in the teaching of an L2 (Swain, 2005). Not many studies have investigated output-based teaching in L2 pragmatics. Tajeddin and Pezeshki (2014) examined the teaching effect on learners' uses of politeness markers using textual enhancement and output tasks that required learners to revise sentences to make them more polite. It was found that the textual enhancement group outperformed the output group in their comprehension and judgment of politeness markers, while the output group improved more than the input group in the production of politeness markers. However, it is worth pointing out that in the output group the learners were also offered explanations about politeness markers in English and examples in their L1, which explicitly provided them with metapragmatic explanation and may have raised their consciousness of the use of politeness markers.

Fakher Ajabshir (2022) compared the effects of output- and input-based teaching on learners' comprehension and production of request modification. After watching short video clips containing target features, the output group learners were required to reconstruct each dialogue so that it was as similar as possible to the video clips. The results indicated that output teaching could yield effects as large as textual enhancement in the learners' pragmatic appropriateness judgment, and better effects in their production than textual enhancement and input flood.

3.2.5 Task-based Pragmatics Teaching

Task-based teaching in L2 pragmatics has been attracting the attention of a group of researchers over the last decade (see González-Lloret, 2019 for a review). Tasks are goal-oriented and meaning-based activities, which simulate authentic communicative contexts. Therefore, tasks can provide opportunities for authentic language practice in the classroom. Gilabert and Barón (2013) investigated the extent to which increasing cognitive task demands affected Spanish/Catalan English learners' pragmatic moves, analyzed by interactions in the use of requests and suggestions. Task complexity was operationalized by [+/- few elements] and [+/- reasoning demands]. The results indicated that the learners produced a larger number of pragmatic moves when performing the complex tasks than the simple tasks. However, task complexity did not influence the learners' uses of the types of request and suggestion strategies, indicating that greater cognitive task demands may not necessarily push learners to use a wider range of pragmatic strategies. The authors suggested that pedagogy intervention prior to task performance might encourage learners to use unfamiliar and more diverse pragmatic moves.

Kim and Taguchi (2015) introduced pragmatic-related episodes (PREs), defined as discussions on, questions about, or corrections of pragmatic production, in analyzing learners' performance while completing tasks. They examined the impact of tasks across different complexity levels on Korean junior high school students' request expressions in English. Task complexity was operationalized as different levels of reasoning demands, following Robinson's (2001) Cognition Hypothesis that more complex tasks promote interaction and language development. In the simple tasks group the learners had detailed scenario descriptions and matching pictures, while in the complex group the learners did not have any detailed description of the scenarios. The findings showed that the learners in the complex task group produced more PREs than those in the simple task group. Both task groups outperformed the control group in terms of request production (request strategies, external and internal modifiers) as measured by DCTs. It is worth pointing out that the learners in both groups were provided with explicit metapragmatic explanation of target pragmatic forms, while the control group was not; it is possible that such explicit pre-task training may have also contributed to the differences between the control and experimental groups. The complex task group did not outperform the simple task group in learning the request expressions in the immediate post-test, but one month after the instruction the complex group performed better than the simple group at retaining their knowledge of the target-mitigated preparatory head act forms.

Kim and Taguchi (2016) expanded their previous work by adding high vs. low pragmatic situational demands with respect to power, social distance, and imposition of ranking of a request. The results showed that collaborative tasks could benefit the learning of pragmatic features; cognitively more complex tasks elicited more interaction based on the number of turns than the simple tasks, regardless of the level of pragmatic task demands. However, the influence was on the learners' discussions of sociopragmatic factors rather than pragma-linguistic forms.

Gilabert and Barón (2018) carried out one of the few studies to examine the possible effect of task sequence. They operationalized four levels of task complexity based on input frequency, familiarity with the interlocutor, casual vs. intentional reasoning, and number of elements. The tasks were presented across two conditions: a simple to complex condition and a randomized condition. The results showed that the judges' perception of task difficulty was in accordance with the difficulty levels predicted by the task design. It was likely that the judges interpreted the difficulty and mental effort of tasks similarly, which caused the authors to argue that only one measurement of difficulty or mental effort may be necessary for future research. In addition, the task sequence (simple to complex vs. randomized) did not influence the learners' pragmatic performance assessed by the judges' rating.

Gomez-Laich (2018) expanded the scope of instructional targets from speech acts in oral communication to written genres, examining the effect of the reasoning demands of tasks on learners' interaction patterns during a collaborative writing task involving persuasion. The simple task group received teaching on rhetoric moves and linguistic resources for persuasive writing, while the complex task group did not receive much assistance. The results showed that the complex task prompted learners to negotiate more over the essay's structure and their sources of difficulty than the simple task. These findings are rather predictable since the difficulties encountered by the complex task group were taught to the simple task group. What would have been more interesting is whether the reasoning demands affected the learners' persuasive writing, but unfortunately this was not analyzed in this study.

The genre of email has also been investigated in task-based pragmatics teaching. Alcón Soler (2018) examined whether interacting with a teacher or another learner would influence learners' use of request mitigators in email tasks. The results revealed that the tasks improved the learners' use of request mitigators, and the participatory structure also influenced their learning outcome. The learners who engaged in student–student interaction paid more attention to pragmatics and enhanced their awareness of mitigation in email requests more than those who engaged in student–teacher interaction. Meanwhile, Levkina (2018) investigated the effect of proficiency and email writing tasks on Spanish EFL learners' judgments of the appropriateness of apologies, justifications, and thanks in students' emails. The results revealed that the two proficiency groups improved their performance after the task-based instruction, but this did not correlate with their proficiency.

The effects of task modalities have also been explored. Tang (2019) examined the effects of computer-mediated communication (CMC) vs. a face-to-face (FTF) condition. The results showed the advantages of FTF on L2 Chinese learners' use of modal verbs. She hypothesized that the frequent use of fragments and symbols in CMC might have constrained opportunities for learners to use proper linguistic forms. Reagan and Payant (2018) examined the influence of oral vs. written tasks on L2 Spanish learners' request strategies and external and internal modification, measured by oral and written DCTs. The results indicated that task-based teaching had positive effects on the learners' development of indirect request head acts and their external and internal modifications. Task modality did not influence the learners' pragmatic development. Again, however, it is worth pointing out that both groups of learners were given explicit teaching on request head acts and modification prior to the task activities. As with Kim and Taguchi's (2015) study, this explicit pre-task teaching may have influenced the learners' performance. In the next subsection, I will examine the effectiveness of explicit teaching on pragmatics.

3.2.6 Explicit Teaching

Second language pragmatics explicit teaching involves metapragmatic explanations of pragmalinguistic uses and/or of the sociopragmatic rules of target pragmatic features, which are often accompanied by various kinds of activities. The benefits of explicit teaching are well documented in the literature (e.g., Halenko, 2021; Rose, 2005; Taguchi, 2011c). For example, Félix-Brasdefer (2008b) examined the effects of explicit instruction on L2 Spanish learners' use of internal modification of refusals. Both the experimental group and the control group carried out a cross-cultural segment comparison activity, but only the experimental group received metapragmatic instruction. The results demonstrated that the experimental group's pragmatic competence improved significantly, as evidenced by more types and a higher frequency of lexical and syntactic mitigators in their refusal responses. The improvement was retained one month after the instruction.

Existing research often compares the effectiveness of explicit and implicit interventions across a wide range of pragmatic features, and most studies have revealed the advantage of explicit teaching over implicit teaching in improving learners' pragmatic competence. For example, Takahashi (2001) compared the improvement of learners' requests in four conditions: explicit metapragmatic teaching, two methods aiming to raise learners' pragmatics consciousness by asking them to compare forms between native speakers' and their own request strategies and to search for native-like request strategies in input, and reading comprehension. The results showed that the three implicit conditions did not yield significant differences, while explicit teaching was the most effective in improving learners' pragmatic competence.

Similarly, Alcón Soler (2005) investigated the effects of explicit instruction versus textual enhancement on Spanish high school EFL learners' English requests. The explicit teaching group received awareness-raising tasks and written metapragmatic feedback related to the use of appropriate requests. The results revealed that both the explicit and the implicit teaching helped the learners to develop their pragmatic awareness with similar effects. However, the explicit teaching had an advantage over implicit teaching with respect to the learners' request production. Meanwhile, Ghobadi and Fahim (2009) compared the effects of explicit and implicit teaching on Iranian EFL learners' pragmatic awareness of thanking. The explicit group were provided with metapragmatic explanations of English thanking strategies and roleplayed conversations in pairs, while the implicit group carried out the roleplays but were not given any explanations. The results showed that the explicit group outperformed the implicit group.

Takimoto (2012) investigated the effects of consciousness raising teaching with and without metapragmatic instruction on Japanese learners' recognition and production of English request downgraders. The results showed that both groups performed significantly better than the control group, and no differences were found between the two groups with respect to pragmatic judgment. However, the explicit teaching group performed better in terms of their production of request downgraders than the implicit teaching group. Finally, in Ahmadian's (2020) study, explicit group learners received descriptions and examples of refusal strategies and were provided with corrective feedback on their incorrect use of refusal strategies in roleplays. The results revealed that explicit instruction was more effective than implicit instruction for both the production and comprehension of refusals.

Researchers have sometimes included several activities in their design. For example, in Eslami *et al.* (2015), for the implicit group the teaching activities included textual enhancement, consciousness-raising activities of requests comparison, production activities using DCTs, and reflection based on recasts and implicit feedback; for the explicit group, the teaching activities included metapragmatic explanation, consciousness-raising by asking learners to provide examples of requests in L1 and L2 and identify request strategies and modification, discussion of inappropriate requests and the potential reasons, production activities, and explicit feedback. The findings revealed that the explicit group improved more than the implicit group in terms of requests, measured by DCTs. However, with so many activities in the two teaching groups, it is difficult to tell which activities led to the different improvements in the two groups.

In contrast, not all studies have demonstrated the advantages of explicit teaching over implicit teaching. Alcón Soler (2007) compared explicit and implicit teaching in terms of learners' awareness of suggestions. The explicit group received metapragmatic explanations and were offered awareness-raising tasks and practices, while the implicit group received textual enhancement of pragmalinguistic aspects and sociopragmatic factors in bold and recast during roleplays. The results revealed that the combination of the two implicit teaching techniques was as effective as the explicit teaching in improving the learners' pragmatic awareness. Hernández (2011) even reported that combining explicit teaching with input flood was not superior to input flood alone in developing learners' use of Spanish discourse markers.

The effect of explicit teaching has also been investigated in different modalities. For example, Fordyce (2014) investigated the effect of explicit and implicit intervention on learners' uses of epistemic stance in writing. The explicit intervention included metapragmatic rule explanation combined with various textual enhancement and awareness-raising activities to direct learners' attention to target forms. The results showed that the explicit intervention clearly had a much greater effect on the learners' use of epistemic features than the implicit intervention, although the development from the explicit intervention decreased from immediate post-test to delayed post-test five months later. Fakher Ajabshir (2019) explored the effect of pragmatic teaching delivered through synchronous and asynchronous CMC versus FTF interaction on learners' acquisition of requests. The teaching activities were the same for the three groups of learners, and included metapragmatic instruction, watching video clips on requests, and discussion and practice with peers. The findings revealed that the CMC-oriented instruction produced better results than the FTF instruction, but no significant difference was found between the asynchronous and synchronous groups. Takimoto (2020) compared the effects of cognitive metaphor with explanation and visualization of the politeness level of requests in terms of spatial concepts versus metapragmatic explanation of politeness level on learners' production and awareness of requests. The results revealed that the cognitive approach outperformed the non-cognitive approach for both production and awareness tasks.

In terms of explicit metapragmatic instruction, the relative advantage of inductive and deductive teaching has also been investigated. For the teaching of pragmatics, deductive teaching refers to the instruction that begins with the provision of metapragmatic information, followed by examples and practice, while in inductive teaching, learners are first presented with examples and exercises containing the pragmatic aspects to be taught, and then are guided to discover or provided with the metapragmatic rules. Glaser (2016) compared inductive and deductive approaches to explicit teaching in the context of EFL learners' use of refusal strategies and adjuncts. The results revealed an advantage of inductive explicit teaching over deductive explicit teaching in teaching refusals in English. The superiority of inductive explicit instruction over deductive explicit instruction is echoed in Qi and Lai's (2017) study, which examined the teaching of requests to L2 Chinese learners via a self-access website. Likewise, Haghighi *et al.* (2019) found an advantage of metapragmatic explanation with inductive teaching over deductive teaching in Iranian EFL learners' use of refusals, although they compared flipped classroom and conventional classroom.

Finally, assessment methods may yield different results, even if learners receive the same teaching. For example, Taylor (2002) offered learners metapragmatic teaching and practice in learning gambits in Spanish, testing their performance by either discussion tasks or roleplay tasks. The study found that the discussion group showed a significant increase in the variety of gambits they used after instruction, whereas the roleplay group did not.

3.3 Summary

The above sections demonstrate that pragmatics teaching contributes to learners' pragmatic development, whether in more salient aspects such as pragmatic routines and speech act strategies or less salient aspects such as internal modifiers of speech acts. Therefore, the first question about whether pragmatic teaching is effective is often treated as a prerequisite for further investigation in L2 pragmatics teaching. As reviewed in this section, there are now fairly well-established teaching frameworks that have been found to be effective and can be used in bringing pragmatics to the classroom. Researchers now spend their efforts on exploring which approach and methods can bring about better and stronger effects in terms of developing learners' pragmatic competence.

This line of research reveals a much more complex picture. Existing narrative reviews (Kasper and Rose, 1999; Rose, 2005; Taguchi, 2011c), syntheses (Taguchi, 2015b; Takahashi, 2010) and meta-analyses (Jeon and Kaya, 2006; Plonsky and Zhuang, 2019) all point to the superiority of explicit teaching interventions over implicit teaching. However, they also acknowledge that factors such as target pragmatic features, learner characteristics, and different degrees of the teaching method, along implicitness–explicitness and length of instruction, all have impacts on the efficacy of L2 pragmatics instruction. In addition, the lack of delayed tests in empirical studies fails to document the sustainability or longevity of instructional effects. Finally, as illustrated by the reviews in this section, many studies combine a wide variety of teaching activities. Quite often the explicit teaching group also receives various implicit teaching activities, particularly aiming to raise learners' awareness of target features. The increasingly popular task-based pragmatics teaching also often includes metapragmatic explanation prior to task activities. Therefore, the findings regarding the efficacy of teaching approaches are far from conclusive, and more research is warranted to further explore this issue.

4 Second Language Pragmatics Assessment

Pragmatics assessment is a crucial but often neglected branch of research in L2 pragmatics, although it dates back at least as far as seminal works by Hudson *et al.* (1992, 1995). One reason for this may be because assessing and measuring pragmatic competence is inherently complex since pragmatics in essence emphasizes dynamic meaning making processes in interaction. It is extremely difficult to capture the fluid and ongoing nature of interaction, particularly in formal and large-scale tests. This section will review this growing field, examining what research on pragmatics assessment has explored and achieved.

4.1 Pragmatic Aspects Assessed

To date, few L2 pragmatics studies explicitly state that they are assessing learners' pragmatic competence. This may be partially due to the fact that assessing learners' pragmatic competence at a certain point is close to measuring their pragmatic production and/or perception, which is the focus of studies on pragmatic learning (see Section 2). There is considerable overlap between these two fields in this sense. Hudson *et al.* (1995) is one of the earliest studies to examine L2 English learners' pragmatic knowledge of apology, request, and refusal using six measures, including open-ended written DCTs, oral DCTs, roleplays, multiple-choice DCTs, and self-assessment rating scales for the DCTs and roleplays. They operationalized the difficulty levels of items according to three sociopragmatic variables from Brown and Levinson's (1987) politeness theory: social status, social distance, and ranking of imposition. A situation with higher social status difference and social distance between the speaker and hearer and a higher ranking for the imposition of a speech act was considered more difficult than a situation with lower levels of these three factors. This way of distinguishing the difficulty levels of items is very influential and has frequently been used in later studies (e.g., Liu, 2007; Taguchi, 2007b; Youn, 2020a).

Compared with speech acts, more studies assess learners' receptive pragmatic knowledge such as their comprehension of conversation implicature. For example, Roever (2005) examined learners' knowledge of implicature and routines using multiple-choice DCTs, with the implicature items adopted from Bouton (1994). Taguchi (2009b) illustrated how she designed multiple-choice items to evaluate learners' comprehension of more and less implicatures in English based on two corpora. She found that comprehension of indirect refusals was easier than comprehension of routines. Questioning a lack of correspondence with empirical conversational data, Walters (2009) showcased the development of a multiple-choice listening test to assess learners' pragmatic comprehension in English, employing findings from conversation analysis. He operationalized learners' pragmatic competence as the ability to understand three types of pragmatic actions: assessment responses, compliment responses, and pre-sequence responses. Walters acknowledged that the three actions did not represent learners' overall pragmatic competence; the reasons for using these three types of actions were simply because they were well documented in the existing conversation analysis literature.

The above approach explicitly assesses learners' pragmatic knowledge as an individual trait, but this has been criticized on the grounds that it fails to uncover learners' pragmatic performance in real interaction. In recent years, many researchers have paid attention to assessing learners' abilities to use language in interaction, often conceptualized as interactional competence (see a collection of studies in Ross and Kasper, 2013). Youn (2020a) investigated how to analyze learners' interactional competence quantitatively. Three interactional features were identified—length of interaction, engaging with interaction, and sequential organization—each consisting of various indices. Although the interactional features functioned differently across different roleplays, they were shown to be useful in operationalizing the construct of L2 pragmatic interaction. In another qualitative study, Youn (2020b) showcased how learners jointly accomplished proposal sequences in roleplays. It was found that lower-level learners often initiated a proposal sequence without establishing a shared understanding relevant to upcoming actions, while higher-level learners typically employed various shift markers and stepwise transition when initiating and shifting actions. When responding to a proposal the higher-level learners recurrently used coherent topic organizations, but in terms of closing a proposal sequence learners across all proficiency levels were able to perform well.

The associations between high-stakes exams and real communication contexts have also been explored. Seedhouse (2013) compared interaction, in terms of repair, sequence organization, and turn taking, in the IELTS Speaking Test (IST) and in L2 classrooms and academic classes at universities. The findings showed that the interaction in the three settings was organized to meet the specific institutional goals. Contrasting with the rigid structure of the IST, the interactional organization of L2 classrooms and university classes varied widely. For example, interviewers in the IST limited repair to clear up test takers' misunderstanding of interview questions, while teachers and peers frequently provided repair, corrections, and evaluation in L2 classrooms and academic classes. Roever and Ikeda (2022) investigated the extent to which the speaking section of the TOEFL iBT could provide information about the test-takers' interactional competence. They asked two raters to evaluate participants' roleplays against four criteria: language use for mitigation, social actions, engagement in interaction, and turn organization. The results suggested that the TOEFL iBT speaking section could only predict testees' ability to use language in interaction to a limited degree. The authors suggested that the absence of recipient design, one of the crucial components of interactional competence, in TOEFL iBT might account for the dissociation between the two measures.

In line with the status quo in L2 pragmatics learning, learners' interaction has rarely been investigated in the written modality (see Section 2.3). Huth and Betz (2019) set out to assess learners' interactional knowledge by testing generic practices of interaction in written formats, for instance, using an unscramble-the-sequence task for testing sequence organization in conversation closings, a multiple-choice completion task for projection in interactional quoting, and data analysis/peer discovery of connectors for repair. The authors argued that testing formats for learners' interactional competence may not necessarily encourage learners to follow prescriptive normativity. Assessing L2 interaction did "not aim for the right answers, but highlight[ed] systematicity, context sensitivity and diversification" (Huth and Betz, 2019: 348).

Dynamic assessment has also been employed to evaluate learners' pragmatic production and comprehension. For example, combining conversation analysis and dynamic assessment, Nicholas (2020) used dynamically administered strategic interaction scenarios (D-SIS) to assess Japanese EFL learners' difficulties and development when requesting during interaction. In a D-SIS the researcher performs one of the roles in a roleplay with the learner. Either the learner or the researcher can pause the task whenever they feel there is a challenging issue and begin a mediation procedure, an insertion sequence initiated after pausing the roleplay. Nicholas distinguished two types of learners' mediation: requiring implicit assistance, indicating that the learner had efficiently oriented to or resolved an object, or extensive explicit mediation, indicating that the object was a particular problem for the learner (van Compernolle, 2013). Thus, by analyzing mediation in the D-SIS, researchers can identify learners' pragmatic difficulties and trace their development in interaction. Qin and van Compernolle (2021) reported on the design and administration of an online dynamic assessment of implicature comprehension in L2 Chinese; learners were classified into beginner, intermediate, and advanced levels, and the assessment was centered on indirect acceptance, refusals, and opinions. The results showed that while all the learners could improve with mediation, individual variation existed in their responsiveness to assistance. The authors claimed that the learners' performances with mediation were more informative than independent performance in terms of assessing their pragmatic competence.

4.2 Validity

Validity is an important aspect of assessment, whether the research targets learners' pragmatic knowledge or interaction. Validation studies aim to systematically investigate empirical evidence that "provides insights into the extent to which a test measures what it is supposed to measure, relative to its purpose and use" (Timpe-Laughlin and Choi, 2017: 21). Haastrup (1986) carried out one of the earliest studies to address this, dealing with the validity issues of assessing pragmatics in a structured oral interview in English with Danish children. Haastrup argued that teachers can engage children in a conversation or a simulation (similar to a roleplay) to assess their pragmatic competence, which was operationalized as the ability to carry out a range of speech acts. The validity of roleplays was analyzed in Youn (2018a, 2020a) based on conversation analysis, showing that carefully designed roleplays can elicit valid interactional data that reflects learners' pragmatic competence.

The validity of different measurements has been compared. Brown (2001) investigated six types of measures in an EFL setting and a Japanese as L2 setting: a written DCT, a multiple-choice DCT, an oral DCT, a roleplay, a discourse self-assessment task, and a roleplay self-assessment. The results showed that the original English versions of the six pragmatics tests generally did not work as well as the Japanese translation versions, in terms of their reliability and the amounts of variance produced. The EFL tests were subject to stronger method effects than the JSL (Japanese as a Second Language) tests. The author discussed the practical advantages and disadvantages of the six types of tests and ranked the EFL and JSL results separately according to each of the following characteristics: easiness to complete, ease of administration and scoring, validity, reliability, variance, encourages oral language and self-reflection, and suitability for high-stakes decision.

Hudson (2001) examined the method effects of written DCTs, oral DCTs, and roleplays on three speech acts: requests, refusals, and apologies. The results showed that oral DCTs were slightly more difficult than roleplays and written DCTs, while roleplays seemed to measure different pragmatic constructs than the two DCTs. This discrepancy between DCTs and more interactive oral measurement techniques was echoed by Walters (2013), who suggested that the oral conversation analysis-informed tests and DCTs did not measure the same construct. Brown (2008) reported reasonably high reliability estimates for the test instruments used in his earlier study (Brown, 2001; Hudson *et al.*, 1995) except for multiple-choice DCTs.

Hinkel (1997) argued that to increase the validity of a multiple-choice task, it must be constructed around actual situations in which the speech act was performed, supplemented by previous relevant research findings on the speech act. In addition, production responses from pilot DCTs should serve as the options for multiple-choice test design and development. These suggestions were adopted by Liu (2007), who developed a multiple-choice DCT to assess Chinese English learners' apologies in five steps. The first was exemplar generation, in which Chinese students were asked to identify situations where apologies were needed. The second step was to check situation likelihood, which explored how likely it was that the situation would occur in the students' life. The third step, metapragmatic assessment, asked the students to assess the sociopragmatic variables in each scenario. In the fourth step the scenarios were validated. Finally, multiple-choice options were developed by including alternative responses collected from students' DCTs. The results of both Rasch analysis and learners' verbal reports showed that the multiple-choice DCT was reliable and valid.

The validity of DCTs has been examined and challenged for a long time. They have been criticized for having low construct validity, since they cannot collect data representing the oral features of authentic discourse (Golato, 2003; Johnston *et al.*, 1998; Rose, 1994). For example, examining advice among English native speakers and Chinese EFL learners, Hinkel (1997) found that

DCTs failed to elicit responses approximating actual speech acts. However, Beebe and Cummings (1996) documented that data elicited with DCTs were consistent with naturally occurring data in terms of main patterns and formulas. Economidou-Kogetsidis (2013) compared written DCT and naturally occurring requests, which found that the written DCT requests approximated natural data in terms of directness and lexical modification. In addition, Billmyer and Varghese (2000) examined the effects of enriching the content of situation prompts in DCTs on L1 and L2 speakers' output. The results showed that the content-enriched prompts elicited more robust external modification and elaboration than content-poor prompts, "in much the same way as speech in natural spontaneous interaction" (Billmyer and Varghese, 2000: 533). This is in line with Beebe and Cummings (1996). However, enriched DCT prompts are often long, which means that learners may find them cognitively demanding and difficult (Roever, 2004).

Cognitive validity in an L2 pragmatics test is occasionally explored by examining what test takers do when completing the test, and whether the cognitive mechanisms involved in their test performances match the construct. Labben (2016) examined the cognitive validity of DCTs and argued that written DCTs should be treated as a language test rather than a questionnaire, and should undergo a rigorous developmental process. Youn and Bi (2019) analyzed learners' reported strategy use in monologic speaking tasks and roleplays to investigate the cognitive validity of L2 pragmatic assessment. They found that higher-level learners were likely to report different types of strategies more frequently than lower-level learners. However, regardless of L2 proficiency levels, learners were aware of the importance of being polite and pragmatically appropriate. Distinct strategies were used depending on the different characteristics of monologic versus dialogic tasks, thus demonstrating that the pragmatic assessment tasks measured the intended constructs and echoing the findings in previous research (e.g., Hudson, 2001).

The above studies focus on assessing learners' production, albeit through measurements that require learners to choose an option for production. Timpe-Laughlin and Choi (2017) aimed to collect evidence of construct validity for a test of receptive pragmatic competence, using a web-based assessment measuring learners' pragmatic comprehension. The test consisted of tasks targeting learners' knowledge of the speech acts of requests and offers, routine formulae, and culture-dependent phrases and idioms. The results were quite positive, indicating that the test scores could reliably measure university students' pragmatic knowledge and provide instructors with useful and meaningful information about the students' receptive pragmatic competence.

4.3 Rating

It is challenging but crucial to develop criteria that measure learners' pragmatic competence. Since appropriateness varies according to contexts and potentially in different raters' reactions, rater disagreement is likely and even expected in pragmatics assessment. Therefore, it is necessary to develop a reliable and valid rating scale to objectively evaluate learners' L2 pragmatic performance.

Several studies developed their rating scales a priori, sometimes with reference to previous literature or a needs analysis (Youn, 2018b). For example, Hudson *et al.* (1995) used five-point scales on six dimensions, asking participants to evaluate learners' production collected by DCTs from very unsatisfactory to completely appropriate; the dimensions included the ability to use the correct speech act, typical expressions, amount of speech and information, and levels of formality, directness, and politeness. Sasaki (1998) asked two trained native speakers to evaluate learners' pragmatic production in DCTs and roleplays in terms of appropriateness and grammar/structure. Although she also used fluency for roleplays, this dimension was not reported. Appropriateness had four levels, ranging from least appropriate/acceptable (scores 1–2), not really appropriate but acceptable (scores 3–5), appropriate to some degree (scores 6–8), and most appropriate for the given situation (scores 9–10) (Sasaki, 1998: 465).

Meanwhile, Taguchi (2007b: 121) used a six-point simplified appropriateness rating scale to ask six native speakers to evaluate learners' performance on a pragmatic speaking task. Specifically, the zero point indicated no performance; a rating of 1 indicated very poor performance, where responses were very difficult to understand and no intended speech acts were performed; a rating of 2 indicated a poor performance, where appropriateness was difficult to judge; a score of 3 indicated a fair performance, where expressions were somewhat appropriate; a score of 4 showed a good performance, where expressions were mostly appropriate; and a score of 5 points indicated an excellent performance, where expressions were fully appropriate. This rating scale has frequently been adopted or adapted in later studies to measure learners' pragmatic performance (e.g., Levkina, 2018; Li, 2014; Taguchi, 2011b). Kuiken and Vedder (2017) developed a six-point rating scale to assess to what extent a text fulfilled the communicative function intended. The rating scale consisted of four dimensions, including content, task requirements, comprehensibility, and coherence and cohesion. Finally, Kley (2019: 318) proposed a rubric for evaluating learners' interactional competence using a three-point rating scale with four criteria: initiating new topics, reciprocating the interlocutor's topic-initiating questions, shifting between topics, and expanding on topics.

Unlike the above ratings analyzing learner responses on different dimensions, Walters (2007) deliberately designed a four-point holistic rating scale to evaluate learners' oral production of assessment responses, compliment responses, and pre-sequence responses. The rubric was vague, with a score of 1 indicating no evidence of control of assessment responses, 2 indicating more evidence of no control, 3 indicating more evidence of control, and a score of 4 indicating evidence of control (Walters, 2007: 168). It is worth noting that Walters stated that the vagueness of the rubric was intentional, given the exploratory nature of applying conversation analysis to rating pragmatic performance.

A couple of studies generated their rating scales based on analyses of learners' pragmatic performance, thereby increasing the validity of the rating scales. Youn (2015) developed five rating categories for interactive open role-plays to be used in classroom assessment in an academic English context, including content delivery, language use, sensitivity to situation, engaging with interaction, and turn organization. Content delivery measures learners' ability to speak appropriately and fluently in a turn; language use measures a range of pragmalinguistic strategies; sensitivity to situation measures the learners' sociopragmatic perceptions and awareness; engaging with interaction measures the degree of learners' engagement and coordination with the interlocutor in roleplays; and turn organization measures learners' orientation to normative turn-taking conventions. Quantitative analyses confirmed the unique contribution of each of the five categories in measuring learners' pragmatic competence in interaction.

Chen and Liu (2016) developed and validated a rating scale to evaluate the speech act performance of apology and request by intermediate Chinese EFL learners in written DCTs. In the scale development stage, initially native speaker raters without training were asked to judge the content and form of DCT productions by American English native speakers and Chinese EFL learners across five hypothesized ability levels, ranging from very poor, poor, fair, good, to excellent along a 10-point Likert scale with a 2-point margin between each level, and write comments for each response. Next, the raters' comments were coded and the DCTs were classified into five sub-corpora consisting of scripts banded into the five hypothesized levels. A detailed analyses of the rater comments and the DCT productions resulted in a rating scale consisting of two 10-point subscales (for a detailed description, see Chen and Liu, 2016: 239). In the validation stage, seven trained raters were asked to rate another group of Chinese EFL learner' email productions, and a FACETS analysis was conducted to examine the validity and reliability of the rating scale. The results showed that the rating scale could reliably differentiate the learners' email production. In terms of validity, the results showed that some levels of the 10-point scale were disordered, and the 2-point interval for each ability level confused the raters because it was difficult for them to tell the difference between the two scores at the same level.

In addition to developing rating scales, researchers have also investigated rater variation in evaluating learners' pragmatic performance. Walters (2007) found that a native English rater and a non-native English rater interpreted learners' performance differently, with the non-native rater paying more attention to fluency and pronunciation than the native speaker rater. Tajeddin and Alemi (2014) investigated native English teachers' ratings of EFL learners' apology DCTs, and whether there was rater bias in their ratings. A content analysis of the raters' descriptions revealed that they mostly paid attention to expressions of apology, explanations, offers of repair, promises for the future, and politeness. Quantitative analyses via FACETS indicated that the raters showed different degrees of severity and tolerance in their ratings.

The influences of raters' cultural and linguistic backgrounds on their ratings have also been explored. Taguchi (2011b) investigated rater variation in the judgment of speech acts by analyzing judges' verbal interview data. Four native English speakers from different cultural backgrounds – one African American, one Asian American and two Australians – assessed the appropriateness of requests and opinions produced by Japanese EFL learners. The findings showed that the raters evaluated the appropriateness of speech acts differently; some focused more on pragmalinguistic aspects such as the directness level of head acts and the use of politeness markers, while others paid more attention to non-linguistic aspects such as the content of politeness strategies. Even when raters focused on the same dimensions of pragmatic performance, they varied in their degree of tolerance – for example, in their level of acceptance of length of low-imposition requests.

Sonnenburg-Winkler *et al.* (2020) carried out one of the few studies exploring the relationship between linguistic background and pragmatics ratings. This study investigated variability among raters from different L1s by asking ten participants to evaluate written request DCTs produced by their peers and themselves using the rating scale developed by Taguchi (2011b). The raters were also asked to provide an explanation for their rating. The findings showed that the raters considered a variety of dimensions when evaluating the speech acts, with some raters focusing more on the directness levels of expressions, while others based their decisions on non-linguistic aspects such as the content of reasons for requests. This finding echoed the rater variation documented in Taguchi (2011b). In addition, raters from the same L1 tended to rate productions produced by speakers of the same L1 similarly.

4.4 Summary

Second language pragmatic assessment is an emerging and crucial field, particularly concerning the validity and reliability in assessing and measuring learners' pragmatic competence in the learning and teaching studies. Validity is indeed one of the key topics in pragmatic assessing research, and the reliability of rating is also an often-examined issue. However, the L2 pragmatic assessing literature should be expanded to explore more issues that are well examined in language assessment but are much neglected in pragmatic assessment, such as washback, assessment literacy, theoretical models, and computer assisted assessment. In addition, learners' cognitive processes during completing tasks are key to understanding their test performance and the cognitive validity of assessment tools. In the next section, the role of cognitive process is discussed as related to pragmatic learning, pragmatic teaching, and pragmatic assessing.

5 Cognitive Processes

The previous sections introduced research on the three fields of L2 pragmatics. This section will analyze studies that explore learners' cognitive processes during pragmatic performance using verbal reports, aiming to identify the major contributions and key methodological concerns related to the use of verbal reports in L2 pragmatics research. Cognitive processes can be investigated alone, or as a part of research to triangulate findings of pragmatic performance. To date, not many studies have examined learners' cognitive processes during pragmatic performance. The following subsections will analyze those studies in detail.

5.1 Instruments to Measure Cognitive Processes in Pragmatics

Verbal reports as a form of introspection solicit verbalization data about the thought processes of participants during the completion of a task (Cohen, 2012; Gass and Mackey, 2016). Verbal reports aim to provide insights into the cognitive processes behind learners' written or spoken behaviors during linguistic performance, which otherwise would have to be investigated indirectly (Cohen, 1998). There are two types of verbal reports: concurrent verbal reports (CVR), also referred to as think aloud protocols, and retrospective verbal reports (RVR), which are implemented subsequent to a task and prompt learners to report on the thoughts they had during task completion. In one of the earliest studies examining learners' cognitive processes in L2 pragmatics, Robinson (1992) showed that when designed and executed with care, particularly in combination with other data collection methods, both CVR and RVR can provide in-depth insights into learners' pragmatic knowledge and their pragmatic difficulties in the planning and execution of speech acts.

Since then a few studies have used CVR, but the majority of the studies on cognitive process in L2 pragmatics have employed RVR. This is understandable as most L2 pragmatics studies examine learners' oral performance, which means they cannot perform CVR simultaneously. RVRs have most often been combined with roleplays (e.g., Cohen and Olshtain, 1993; Woodfield, 2012; Ying and Ren, 2021), but other data collection methods that have been combined with RVRs include conversation elicitation tasks (Nguyen, 2017), comprehension questionnaires (Taguchi, 2008b), written DCTs (Bella, 2014a), and multimedia elicitation tasks (Ren, 2014, 2015). In contrast, CVRs have been combined with various types of questionnaires, including yes/no questions (Taguchi, 2002), appropriateness judgment questionnaires (Timpe-Laughlin *et al.*, 2021), and multiple-choice questionnaires (Chen and Lin, 2021).

Three studies employed both CVR and RVR. Robinson (1992) combined both types of verbal report with DCTs to investigate Japanese English learners' pragmatic knowledge in producing refusals. Woodfield (2010) innovatively explored learners' cognitive processes when they were engaged in DCTs by asking them to conduct verbal reports in pairs. The results showed that paired verbal reports were able to provide insights into learners' cognitive processes and pragmatic knowledge. In addition, paired CVRs were easier and more natural for learners than single-subject CVRs. Following Woodfield (2010), Chen (2015) also combined the two types of verbal report to explore learners' cognitive processes while they were completing an email task.

5.2 Pragmatic Aspects Examined with Cognitive Processes

Research has employed RVRs to investigate learners' cognitive processes during their production of speech acts, among which requests (e.g., Chen, 2015; Cohen and Olshtain, 1993; Woodfield, 2010, 2012) and refusals (e.g., Bella, 2014b; Félix-Brasdefer, 2008a; Ren, 2014) have been the most frequently examined. Other speech acts that have been examined include apology (Bella, 2014a; Cohen and Olshtain, 1993), complaint (Cohen and Olshtain, 1993; Hassall, 2008), criticism and responses (Nguyen, 2017), feedback (Youn and Bi, 2019), greeting responses (Ying and Ren, 2021), and offers (Bella, 2016).

A couple of studies have employed CVRs to explore learners' cognitive processes while they are performing comprehension tasks involving conversational implicature (Chen and Lin, 2021; Taguchi, 2008b). Timpe-Laughlin and

Cho (2021) used CVRs to investigate the effectiveness of a learning platform in developing EFL learners' awareness of requests and offers.

5.3 Verbal Report Data Examined

Most L2 pragmatics research on cognitive processes has collected and analyzed data based on Newell and Simon's (2019 [1972]) theory of problem-solving (e.g., Ren, 2015; Woodfield, 2010) in order to explore the three types of problem-solving processing posited by the model: orient, solve, and evaluation. The first of these, orientation, is often investigated by asking about learners' cognition or attention through questions such as: What did you notice about the situation? What were you paying attention to? What were you focusing on? (e.g., Alcón Soler, 2012; Ren, 2014; Woodfield, 2010). Second, solution is often investigated by asking about learners' intentions or planning through questions such as: What did you intend to convey? (Chen, 2015) What were you trying to achieve? (Bella, 2016) Why did you choose the answer? (Taguchi, 2008b) What made you reply in this manner? (Ren, 2014) To what extent was it important for you to be direct or indirect when you replied in this situation? (Ren, 2015) Can you explain your decision-making process? (e.g., Alcón Soler, 2012; Félix-Brasdefer, 2008a). The third stage, evaluation, is often investigated by asking learners to evaluate the appropriateness of their own pragmatic performance through questions such as: Were you satisfied with your answer? (Alcón Soler, 2012; Woodfield, 2010) How would you evaluate your performance in ... ? (Chen, 2015; Ying and Ren, 2021).

Some studies have been interested in learners' language of thought, asking learners to report on the language they used in planning and executing their performance (e.g., Félix-Brasdefer, 2008a; Ren, 2015; Woodfield, 2010). In addition, studies have explored learners' difficulties and strategy use (e.g., Ren, 2014; Youn and Bi, 2019) in completing pragmatic tasks based on the collected data.

5.4 Procedures of Verbal Report

When learners are asked to report their cognitive processes, either by CVR or RVR, they must be offered training and allowed to practice. Researchers should ask learners specific questions and avoid asking them cognitively complex questions. For example, questions asking learners to explain complicated issues or to compare abstract concepts such as "Which social parameter carries more weight?" should be avoided.

The time span between RVR and pragmatic tasks, whether they are production or perception tasks, should be kept as short as possible. The majority of L2 pragmatics studies conduct RVR immediately after the pragmatic task, which is highly recommended. In cases where RVR cannot be conducted immediately, it is suggested that it should be carried out within two days (Ericsson and Simon, 1993). In addition, learners' performance in the pragmatic task should be replayed to them to help them recall what they did during the task. Researchers should avoid checking learners' memories, since questions asking learners to recall what they were thinking during data collection in the past can cause a serious validity threat. If researchers wish to investigate changes in learners' cognitive processes, RVRs should be conducted after each session, as in Ren (2014). It is not recommended to conduct RVR only in the last phase of data collection if the intention is to explore pragmatic variation across different phases, as Woodfield (2010) admits in her discussion of limitations.

With respect to the mode of RVR, Hernández and Boero (2018) carried out the only study to date that asked learners to write down their thoughts while they were completing pragmatic tasks. As writing is usually much slower than speaking and only offers learners the chance to access their conscious thoughts, it may involve further threats to validity. Future research could investigate the effects of modality on the data collected by verbal report.

5.5 Summary

Verbalization of learners' cognitive processes can provide insights into the reasoning and thought processes behind their performance (e.g., production of certain pragmatic features, awareness of speech acts, and comprehension of implicature). When carefully designed, verbal report data on learners' cognitive process can reveal useful information including the pragmatic difficulties they encounter, the source of knowledge they have, the perception of different instruction approaches and measurement tools, and whether their performance resulted from the lack of pragmatic development or their pragmatic agency. Therefore, investigating learners' cognitive process during pragmatic activities can provide added value for advancing our understanding of L2 pragmatic development. In sum, cognitive process research can integrate studies on learning, teaching, and assessing different aspects of learners' pragmatic production and perception to provide a comprehensive picture of L2 pragmatic competence.

6 Case Studies

This section presents two projects in progress, both focusing on pragmatic production (Section 2.1). The first case study explores advanced L2 Chinese learners' self-praise on social media, in which, in addition to linguistic resource, learners' semiotic and multimodal resources are also included in coding self-praise strategies. The second case study investigates ethnic minority children's pragmatic competence, which challenges the concept of monolingual native speakers in L2 pragmatics and provides more empirical data to research on children's pragmatic development. In showcasing these two studies, we call for more research on L2 pragmatics on social media and on lingua franca pragmatics among children.

6.1 Case Study 1: Second Language Self-praise on Social Media

As discussed in Section 2.3, L2 pragmatics has mainly focused on oral communication, with communication in other modalities being examined less frequently. The field needs to expand its research scope to include more pragmatic features, particularly concerning semiotic and multimodal resources. It is important to examine whether L2 learners can successfully achieve meaning making on social media with the increasingly universal digital affordance. Against this background, I designed a project to investigate instances of self-praise posted on social media by advanced learners of Chinese. Self-praise is a speech act through which interlocutors present positive content of themselves such as appearance, possession, and skills (Ren and Guo, 2020). The reason why self-praise was chosen as the research target is that the phenomenon is pervasive in individuals' daily lives as well as on social media, but it has not been examined from an L2 pragmatics perspective.

Participants and Data

Data were collected from twenty advanced learners of Chinese, who were asked to share self-praise they posted on WeChat Friend, a popular social media platform in China. The learners were aged from twenty to twenty-six years old ($M = 21.42$, $SD = 1.29$), of whom nine were from Thailand, seven from Indonesia, and two each from Mongolia and Laos. They had studied in China for more than three and a half years at the time of data collection and were enrolled in advanced Chinese classes at a university in South China. They contributed different numbers of self-praise instances, ranging from one to five. Altogether sixty-one posts containing instances of self-praise in L2 Chinese were collected from the learners.

To provide a comparison dataset, I also collected 200 self-praise posts from WeChat Friend from 46 Chinese native speaker volunteers aged from nineteen to twenty-five ($M = 21.8$, $SD = 1.622$) who were studying in various universities across China.

Data Analysis

The self-praise posts were analyzed in terms of different pragmatic strategies based on the coding scheme developed by Ren and Guo (2020), with considerations of linguistic, semiotic, and multimodal resources used in the posts. The self-praise posts were read through in several rounds and coded into three major categories: explicit self-praise without modification, modified explicit self-praise, and implicit self-praise. Instances of modified explicit self-praise were further coded into change of praise focus, collectivism, comparison of oneself between one aspect and another, comparison of oneself between past and present, comparison between oneself and others, disclaimer, praise from a third party, and reference to hard work; implicit self-praise instances were further coded into self-praise as a complaint, self-praise as a narration, and self-praise as sharing (see Ren and Guo, 2020 for definitions and examples of each coding).

During the data coding process it was found that some posts contained a mixture of strategies. In such cases, each independent self-praise strategy received a separate coding. Consequently, the 61 self-praise posts shared by the advanced L2 Chinese learners yielded a total of 64 self-praise strategies, and the 200 self-praise posts shared by the Chinese native speakers yielded 205 self-praise strategies.

Two researchers coded the self-praise posts to establish the interrater reliability of the coding. The agreement percentage was 98.36 percent with a kappa coefficient of 0.943, indicating a high interrater reliability.

Results

Due to space limitations, the results can only be introduced very briefly, without delving into statistical analyses and qualitative examinations related to each self-praise strategy. Table 1 presents the frequency and percentage of all the self-praise strategies across the two groups.

As shown in Table 1, on WeChat Friend, which is accessible to the user's real-life WeChat friends, the L2 learners preferred praising themselves explicitly without modification (48.44%) (e.g., "I feel like a star."), followed by modified self-praise (29.69%) (e.g., "A lot of people say that I'm very smart.") and implicit self-praise (21.87%) (e.g., "How annoying! Why do others only see my lovely face but do not know that I also have a smart brain behind it?). In contrast, the Chinese native speakers tended to use implicit self-praise much more frequently (45.86%), followed by explicit self-praise without modification (30.24%) and with modification (23.90%).

It is possible that the learners had not fully developed their pragmatic competence, which led to the divergence of the two groups' self-praise.

Table 1 Frequency and percentage of self-praise strategies

Self-praise strategies	L2 users (Total post = 61)		Native speakers (Total post = 200)	
	Frequency	Percentage	Frequency	Percentage
Explicit self-praise without modification	**31**	**48.44**	**62**	**30.24**
Modified self-praise	**19**	**29.69**	**49**	**23.90**
Change of praise focus	*1*	*1.56*	*12*	*5.85*
Collectivism	*1*	*1.56*	*3*	*1.46*
Comparison between aspects of oneself	*8*	*12.50*	*0*	*0*
Comparison between past and present	*1*	*1.56*	*5*	*2.44*
Comparison between oneself and others	*2*	*3.13*	*0*	*0*
Disclaimer	*0*	*0*	*1*	*0.49*
Praise from a third party	*6*	*9.38*	*15*	*7.32*
Reference to hard work	*0*	*0*	*13*	*6.34*
Implicit self-praise	**14**	**21.87**	**94**	**45.86**
Self-praise as complaint	*2*	*3.13*	*2*	*0.98*
Self-praise as narration	*11*	*17.18*	*4*	*1.95*
Self-praise as sharing	*1*	*1.56*	*88*	*42.93*
Total	**64**	**100**	**205**	**100**

However, it is also possible that the learners would like to perform their agency in the way of positively presenting themselves. Future studies need to include retrospective verbal reports (see Section 5) or interviews to explore whether the (non-)employment of certain strategies resulted from learners' agency or lack of sociopragmatic and pragmalinguistic knowledge. In this case study, the learners had all been studying abroad in China for a few years. As Chinese universities provide dormitories specifically for international students (Ren, 2018a), it is likely that the learners had forged a group of WeChat friends of whom the majority were international students. They might have formed a local group ritual of posting for clarity (Ren, 2014) and explicitly sharing happiness, ease, and positive aspects of life.

This case study exemplifies the benefits of investigating social media communication. Researchers have highlighted the importance of exploring authentic data with real-life consequences (Bardovi-Harlig and Hartford, 2005; Félix-Brasdefer and Cohen, 2012), which cannot be achieved using DCTs and roleplays. Social media presents researchers with an ideal platform in this sense. In addition, more research on pragmatic aspects of social media communication, which have previously been investigated in oral communication, can shed light on the similarities and differences between face-to-face and social media communication in terms of learner pragmatic competence.

6.2 Case Study 2: Lingua Franca Pragmatics

Lingua franca pragmatics refers to the pragmatic practice of ethnic minority people in their national lingua franca. It is different from pragmatics in English as a lingua franca (e.g., Ren, 2018b). As pointed out earlier, L2 pragmatics has predominantly examined adult learners. Children's pragmatic competence, particularly that of ethnic minority children in a multilingual country or area, has rarely been explored. Therefore, I developed a project to investigate Chinese ethnic minority children's pragmatic competence in Mandarin, the national lingua franca in China. I collected data from local children in primary schools, junior high schools, and senior high schools in ethnic minority areas in China including Xinjiang, Tibet, and Inner Mongolia. Due to space limitations, here I only report on one study examining Uyghur-Mandarin children's pragmatic competence when giving advice in written communication, to provide more data to the under-researched written pragmatic competence (see Section 2.3).

Participants and Data

A total of 200 children participated in this case study: 100 bilingual Uyghur-Mandarin children, and 100 monolingual Han-Mandarin children, equally distributed according to gender. The Uyghur-Mandarin children were aged from ten to thirteen years (M = 11.64, SD = 1.14), and all were learning Mandarin as the national lingua franca in their formal schooling context. The Han children were also aged between ten and thirteen years (M = 11.46, SD = 1.08), but they had learned Mandarin as their L1. The 200 participants were all sixth-grade students in elementary schools in the Xinjiang Uygur Autonomous Region of China at the time of data collection.

The study was purposefully designed to investigate the children's ability to write a note. Therefore, a written DCT was used to elicit the speech act of advice. To ensure that the children could understand the task, the scenario was designed to be familiar within the context of the children's life; it presented a situation where a child's mother was trying to lose weight by eating vegetables alone every day. The children were required to write a note to their mother and advise her to change her unhealthy diet.

Data Analysis

The children's responses were coded according to content-based categories, with reference to previous literature (DeCapua and Dunham, 2007; Hampel, 2015). After several rounds of careful reading and coding, the children's responses were coded into advice strategies and supportive moves. The advice strategies consisted of admonition and solution (further divided into single choice and alternatives), while the supportive moves were coded into four types including assessment, compromise, rationale, and affective expression, with the last one being further divided into pleading, warning, complimentary, and encouraging.

Two researchers coded the children's responses to ensure the reliability of the data. The agreement percentage was 96.42 percent with a kappa coefficient of 0.829, which indicated a high interrater reliability.

Results

Table 2 shows the frequency and percentage of each advice strategy and supportive move used by the Uyghur-Mandarin children and the Han children.

As shown in Table 2, the Uyghur-Mandarin children and the Han children revealed a similar profile with respect to the advice strategies and supportive moves they used while writing a note to their mother in this hypothetical situation. The Uyghur-Mandarin used slightly more advice strategies and fewer supportive moves than the Han children (134 vs. 121 and 139 vs. 147, respectively). In terms of specific advice strategies, the Uyghur-Mandarin children used more admonition strategies than the Han children, but the

Table 2 Frequency and percentage of advice strategies and supportive moves

	Uyghur		Han	
	Frequency	**Percentage**	**Frequency**	**Percentage**
Advice Strategies	**134**	**49.08**	**121**	**45.15**
Admonition	52	19.05	38	14.18
Solution	82	30.04	83	30.97
Single choice	*51*	*18.68*	*44*	*16.42*
Alternatives	*31*	*11.36*	*39*	*14.55*
Supportive Moves	**139**	**50.92**	**147**	**54.85**
Assessment	44	16.12	39	14.55
Compromise	13	4.76	17	6.34
Rationale	62	22.71	68	25.37
Affective expression	20	7.33	23	8.58
Pleading	*2*	*0.73*	*0*	*0*
Warning	*13*	*4.76*	*19*	*7.09*
Compliment	*5*	*1.83*	*0*	*0*
Encouraging	*0*	*0*	*4*	*1.49*
Total	**273**	**100**	**268**	**100**

difference was not significant (p = 0.59). The two groups of children used similar numbers of solution strategies, although they showed different preferences in offering single choices or alternatives. The Uyghur-Mandarin children used single choices more frequently and alternatives less frequently than the Han children (51 vs. 44 and 31 vs. 39, respectively), but the differences were not significant.

With respect to supportive moves, it was interesting to note that, when showing affection toward their mother, the Uyghur-Mandarin children used pleading and compliments, but the Han children did not use these two types of supportive moves; on the other hand, the Han children used more warnings and encouragement than the Uyghur-Mandarin children. These findings indicate that the Uyghur-Mandarin preferred to show more involvement politeness to their mothers while writing the advice note than the Han children, who paid more attention to their mothers' independence politeness (Ren and Woodfield, 2016; Scollon and Scollon, 2001). However, this finding warrants more exploration, as the dataset was rather small and the findings were far from conclusive.

Overall, the results revealed more similarities than differences between the ethnic minority children and the monolingual native speaker children. The bilingual ethnic minority children had much more in common with the native speaker children than the advanced L2 learners documented in Case Study 1 and in the previous literature. Case Study 2 exemplifies the need to investigate lingua franca pragmatics, which has been neglected in L2 pragmatics. Lingua franca pragmatics is different from foreign/second language pragmatics, heritage pragmatics, and pragmatics in English as a lingua franca. Ethnic minority children learn a nationally dominant language not only as their L2 but also as the national lingua franca, which is of significant importance if they wish to communicate with the majority community, and crucially it is also owned by them. Therefore, they are highly motivated to learn the language and invest their own agency in using it to perform their identities. Investigating lingua franca pragmatics will provide a novel and comprehensive understanding of L2 pragmatic competence and development. This case study asked the children to write in Mandarin Chinese, their lingual franca; future studies may explore the children's entire linguistic repertoires and their translanguaging competence in pragmatic practice. Indeed, pragmatics of young language learners is a particularly under-studied area within L2 pragmatics (but see Cekaite, 2017; Lee, 2010; Rose, 2000; Savić *et al.*, 2021; Schauer, 2019 for some exceptions), which deserves more attention in the field.

7 Advancing Second Language Pragmatics

As the above sections have shown, L2 pragmatics covers many topics in learning, teaching, and assessing, and investigates a range of pragmatic aspects and possible influential factors. This section will only point out a few potential areas to advance L2 pragmatics research.

Second language pragmatics research tends to investigate specific areas of pragmatic competence (see Section 2) among different learners, which makes the generalization of different studies difficult or even impossible since learners differ across many variables. Although questions concerning commonality versus particularity of pragmatic development and the relation between productive and receptive pragmatic competences have been raised for more than two decades (Kasper and Schmidt, 1996), not many studies have been designed to address such issues. Future research should investigate the interactions among learners' different pragmatic sub-competences (production, perception, and cognition), and explore their pragmatic competence across different layers at micro (immediate interactional contexts), meso (local communicative norms or rituals), and macro (sociocultural systems) levels (Ren, 2019a), as illustrated in Figure 2.

Some particular topics awaiting further exploration include: whether changes in cognitive processes correspond to development in pragmatic performance; whether learners' pragmatic development can be sustained after intervention,

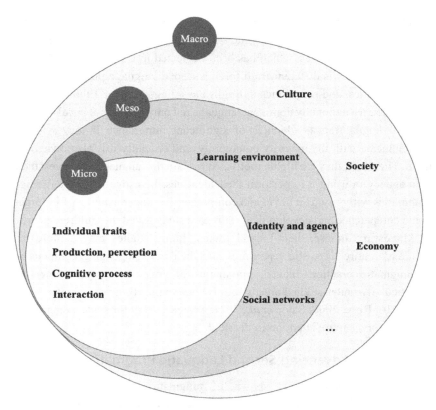

Figure 2 Layers of L2 pragmatics research

whether through learning environment (e.g., study abroad) or pedagogical instruction, and the reasons underlying such results; the usefulness of interventions for learners' pragmatic development and how the development can be facilitated and assessed, particularly if L2 culture contradicts learners' identities or if other factors inhibit their pragmatic learning; and finally, how to link findings in L2 pragmatics learning, teaching, and assessing. To date, L2 pragmatics has mostly examined university students. Future research should investigate more types of learners, including but not restricted to younger learners, and learners at beginner and advanced levels.

The field will benefit from further well-designed studies from a wider range of L1 background and L2 target languages to explore learners' individual differences (see Takahashi, 2019 for a review), investigating not only their difficulties in using an L2 to achieve pragmatic goals, but also how they achieve their desires by using the pragmatic resources available to them (refer to the three components of pragmatic competence

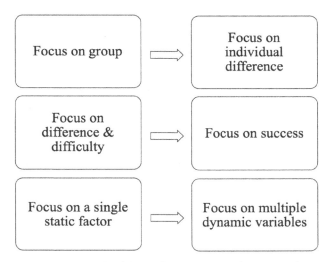

Figure 3 Shift of focus for L2 pragmatics research

in Section 1). In addition, future research should shift from examining one factor at a time to the simultaneous investigation of multiple dynamic variables, to investigate possible interactions between different variables. Sophisticated statistical methods such as multivariable analysis and Structural Equation Modeling will be useful here. Figure 3 illustrates the focus shift for future research.

Another important area is learners' own understanding of their pragmatics performance and development. Assessment-based pragmatic performance alone is not sufficient. Methods such as verbal reports should be included to triangulate not only what learners can really achieve, but also what motives and meaning are assigned to their performance. In addition, social network analysis may provide illuminating insights into factors influencing learners' pragmatic learning and behaviors (e.g., Li *et al.*, 2021).

With respect to pragmatics teaching, as reviewed in Section 3, future research should focus on how to teach pragmatics more effectively and efficiently, rather than on whether pragmatics could or should be taught. Length of instruction, instructional delivery, as well as multiple delayed test stages to determine at what point the benefits of instruction start to wane are underexplored and warrant more specific attention. The majority of L2 pragmatics teaching studies have been conducted in face-to-face contexts. It is vital to investigate how to develop learners' pragmatic competence via technology (see González-Lloret, 2021 for a recent review), particularly in the context of the COVID-19 crisis. It is encouraging that some studies have already explored this issue (e.g., Blyth and Sykes, 2020; Taguchi and Sykes, 2013), but it is worth further exploring how to design tasks using technology to assist learners developing pragmatic competence out of class. Also, Bardovi-Harlig *et al.* (2017) showed the positive effect of using a corpus on learners' oral production and comprehension of pragmatic routines. They highlighted the importance of providing guidance and consciousness-raising activities for learners. However, corpora with annotations for pragmatic categories are still rare. It will be illuminating to explore how teachers can train learners to use the various corpora that are available to improve their pragmatic competence, and how to assess their learning and improvement during this process.

A final aspect is related to offering legitimacy for learners to employ all their available multilingual, multi-semiotic, and multimodal resources in their trans-languaging practice (García and Li, 2014). As being multilingual is increasingly accepted as the norm rather than an exception, multilingual learners should be treated as a whole person (García *et al.*, 2021). Therefore, researchers should revisit the methodological assumptions of the conventional research methods in L2 pragmatics that analyze pragmatic strategies separately in quantifiable codes and compare learners' performance against the monolingual native speaker norm, particularly in fields such as lingua franca pragmatics (see Case Study 2). Rather, L2 pragmatics will develop further by moving forward to investigate learners' pragmatic competence in a dynamic, complex, and inter-active perspective to advance our understanding of the principles and mechan-isms of pragmatic development. In addition, more empirical studies are warranted to explore how to codify learners' translanguaging strategies in interaction (see Case Study 1). It remains to be seen how such practices will come to be acknowledged in foreign language classrooms and large-scale high-stakes exams. A comprehensive coding scheme of learners' translanguaging strategies will indeed help in this aspect. To conclude, the definition and construct of pragmatic competence consisting of linguistic, semiotic and multi-modal resources and knowledge can help to push the boundaries of L2 pragmatics.

References

Achiba, M. 2003. *Learning to request in a second language: A study of child interlanguage pragmatics*. Clevedon: Multilingual Matters.

Ahmadian, M. J. 2020. Explicit and implicit instruction of refusal strategies: Does working memory capacity play a role? *Language Teaching Research*, 24, 163–188.

Alcón Soler, E. 2005. Does instruction work for learning pragmatics in the EFL context? *System*, 33, 417–435.

Alcón Soler, E. 2007. Developing pragmatic awareness of suggestions in the EFL classroom: A focus on instructional effects. *Canadian Journal of Applied Linguistics*, 10, 47–76.

Alcón Soler, E. 2012. Teachability and bilingualism effects on third language learners' pragmatic knowledge. *Intercultural Pragmatics*, 9, 511–541.

Alcón Soler, E. 2018. Effects of task supported language teaching on learners' use and knowledge of email request mitigators. In Taguchi, N. and Kim, Y. (eds.), *Task-based approaches to teaching and assessing pragmatics*. Amsterdam: John Benjamins, 55–82.

Alcón Soler, E. and Sánchez-Hernández, A. 2017. Learning pragmatic routines during study abroad: A focus on proficiency and type of routine. *Atlantis*, 39, 191–210.

Al-Ali, M. N. and Alawneh, R. 2010. Linguistic mitigating devices in American and Jordanian students' requests. *Intercultural Pragmatics*, 7, 311–339.

Allami, H. and Naeimi, A. 2011. A cross-linguistic study of refusals: An analysis of pragmatic competence development in Iranian EFL learners. *Journal of Pragmatics*, 43, 385–406.

Alsuhaibani, Z. 2020. Developing EFL students' pragmatic competence: The case of compliment responses. *Language Teaching Research*, 1–20.

Badjadi, N. E. I. 2016. A meta-analysis of the effects of instructional tasks on L2 pragmatics comprehension and production. In Tang, S. F. and Logonnathan, L. (eds.), *Assessment for learning within and beyond the classroom*. Singapore: Springer, 241–268.

Bardovi-Harlig, K. 2005. Contextualizing interlanguage pragmatics. In Tyler, A., Takada, M., Kim, Y. and Marinova, D. (eds.), *Language in use: Cognitive and discourse perspectives on language and language learning*. Washington, DC: Georgetown University Press, 65–84.

Bardovi-Harlig, K. 2008. Recognition and production of formulas in L2 pragmatics. In Han, Z. (ed.), *Understanding second language process*. Clevedon: Multilingual Matters, 205–222.

Bardovi-Harlig, K. 2009. Conventional expressions as a pragmalinguistic resource: Recognition and production of conventional expressions in L2 pragmatics. *Language Learning*, 59, 755–795.

Bardovi-Harlig, K. 2012. Formulas, routines, and conventional expressions in pragmatics research. *Annual Review of Applied Linguistics*, 32, 206–227.

Bardovi-Harlig, K. 2014. Awareness of meaning of conventional expressions in second-language pragmatics. *Language Awareness*, 23, 41–56.

Bardovi-Harlig, K. 2018. Matching modality in L2 pragmatics research design. *System*, 75, 13–22.

Bardovi-Harlig, K. and Bastos, M.-T. 2011. Proficiency, length of stay, and intensity of interaction, and the acquisition of conventional expressions in L2 pragmatics. *Intercultural Pragmatics*, 8, 347–384.

Bardovi-Harlig, K. and Dörnyei, Z. 1998. Do language learners recognize pragmatic violations? Pragmatic versus grammatical awareness in instructed L2 learning. *TESOL Quarterly*, 32, 233–263.

Bardovi-Harlig, K. and Griffin, R. 2005. L2 pragmatic awareness: Evidence from the ESL classroom. *System*, 33, 401–415.

Bardovi-Harlig, K. and Hartford, B. 1993. Learning the rules of academic talk: A longitudinal study of pragmatic development. *Studies in Second Language Acquisition*, 15, 279–304.

Bardovi-Harlig, K. and Hartford, B. 2005. Institutional discourse and interlanguage pragmatics research. In Bardovi-Harlig, K. and Hartford, B. (eds.), *Interlanguage pragmatics: Exploring institutional talk*. Mahwah, NJ: Lawrence Erlbaum, 7–36.

Bardovi-Harlig, K., Mossman, S., and Su, Y. 2017. The effect of corpus-based instruction on pragmatic routines. *Language Learning & Technology*, 21, 76–103.

Bardovi-Harlig, K. and Su, Y. 2018. The acquisition of conventional expressions as a pragmalinguistic resource in Chinese as a foreign language. *The Modern Language Journal*, 102, 732–757.

Bardovi-Harlig, K. and Vellenga, H. E. 2012. The effect of instruction on conventional expressions in L2 pragmatics. *System*, 40, 77–89.

Barón, J. and Ortega, M. 2018. Investigating age differences in e-mail pragmatic performance. *System*, 78, 148–158.

Barón Parés, J. L. 2012. "Please, please, please": Trying to be polite in an EFL context. In Amaya, L. F., López, M. D. L. O. H., Morón, R. G., *et al.* (eds.),

New perspectives on (im)politeness and interpersonal communication. Newcastle upon Tyne: Cambridge Scholars Publishing, 174–197.

Barón Parés, J. L. 2015. "Can I make a party, mum?" The development of requests from childhood to adolescence. *Atlantis*, 37, 179–198.

Barron, A. 2003. *Acquisition in interlanguage pragmatics: Learning how to do things with words in a study abroad context.* Amsterdam: John Benjamins.

Barron, A. 2019. Using corpus-linguistic methods to track longitudinal development: Routine apologies in the study abroad context. *Journal of Pragmatics*, 146, 87–105.

Barron, A. and Black, E. 2015. Constructing small talk in learner-native speaker voice-based telecollaboration: A focus on topic management and back-channeling. *System*, 48, 112–128.

Béal, C. 1994. Keeping the peace: A cross-cultural comparison of questions and requests in Australian English and French. *Multilingua*, 13, 35–58.

Beebe, L. M. and Cummings, M. 1996. Natural speech data versus written questionnaire data: How data collection method affects speech act performance. In Gass, S. and Neu, J. (eds.), *Speech acts across cultures: Challenges to communication in a second language.* Berlin: Mouton de Gruyter, 65–86.

Beebe, L. M., Takahashi, T., and Uliss-Weltz, R. 1990. Pragmatic transfer in ESL refusals. In Scarcella, R. C., Anderson, E. and Krashen, S. D. (eds.), *Developing communicative competence in a second language.* Rowley, MA: Newbury House, 55–73.

Bell, N., Shardakova, M., and Shively, R. L. 2021. The DCT as a data collection method for L2 humor production. In Félix-Brasdefer, J. C. and Shively, R. L. (eds.), *New directions in second language pragmatics.* Berlin: Mouton de Gruyter, 156–178.

Bella, S. 2011. Mitigation and politeness in Greek invitation refusals: Effects of length of residence in the target community and intensity of interaction on non-native speakers' performance. *Journal of Pragmatics*, 43, 1718–1740.

Bella, S. 2012a. Pragmatic awareness in a second language setting: The case of L2 learners of Greek. *Multilingua*, 31, 1–33.

Bella, S. 2012b. Pragmatic development in a foreign language: A study of Greek FL requests. *Journal of Pragmatics*, 44, 1917–1947.

Bella, S. 2014a. A contrastive study of apologies performed by Greek native speakers and English learners of Greek as a foreign language. *Pragmatics*, 24, 679–713.

Bella, S. 2014b. Developing the ability to refuse: A cross-sectional study of Greek FL refusals. *Journal of Pragmatics*, 61, 35–62.

Bella, S. 2016. Offers by Greek FL learners: A cross-sectional developmental study. *Pragmatics*, 26, 531–562.

Belz, J. A. and Kinginger, C. 2002. The cross-linguistic development of address form use in telecollaborative language learning: Two case studies. *The Canadian Modern Language Review*, 59, 189–214.

Billmyer, K. and Varghese, M. 2000. Investigating instrument-based pragmatic variability: Effects of enhancing discourse completion tests. *Applied Linguistics*, 21, 517–552.

Blattner, G. and Fiori, M. 2012. Virtual social network communities: An investigation of language learners' development of sociopragmatic awareness and multiliteracy skills. *CALICO Journal*, 29, 24–43.

Blood, R. 2018. "When you speak to a police officer and (call them) du": Examining the impact of short-term study abroad on Australian students' awareness of address forms in German. *Study Abroad Research in Second Language Acquisition and International Education*, 3, 117–143.

Blum-Kulka, S., House, J., and Kasper, G. (eds.) 1989. *Cross-cultural pragmatics: Requests and apologies*. Norwood, NJ: Ablex.

Blyth, C. and Sykes, J. M. 2020. Technology-enhanced L2 instructional pragmatics. *Language Learning & Technology*, 24, 1–7.

Bouton, L. F. 1994. Conversational implicature in the second language: Learned slowly when not deliberately taught. *Journal of Pragmatics*, 22, 157–167.

Brown, J. D. 2001. Pragmatics tests: Different purposes, different tests. In Rose, K. R. and Kasper, G. (eds.), *Pragmatics in language teaching*. Cambridge: Cambridge University Press, 301–325.

Brown, J. D. 2008. Raters, functions, item types and the dependability of L2 pragmatics tests. In Alcón Soler, E. and Martínez-Flor, A. (eds.), *Second language acquisition: Investigating pragmatics in foreign language learning, teaching and testing*. Bristol: Multilingual Matters, 224–248.

Brown, L. 2013. Identity and honorifics use in Korean study abroad. In Kinginger, C. (ed.), *Social and cultural aspects of language learning in study abroad*. Amsterdam: John Benjamins, 269–298.

Brown, P. and Levinson, S. C. 1987. *Politeness: Some universals in language usage*. Cambridge: Cambridge University Press.

Buysse, L. 2012. *So* as a multifunctional discourse marker in native and learner speech. *Journal of Pragmatics*, 44, 1764–1782.

Buysse, L. 2015. "Well it's not very ideal … " the pragmatic marker *well* in learner English. *Intercultural Pragmatics*, 12, 59–89.

Cekaite, A. 2017. What makes a child a good language learner? Interactional competence, identity, and immersion in a Swedish classroom. *Annual Review of Applied Linguistics*, 37, 45–61.

Chang, Y.-F. 2010. "I no say you say is boring": The development of pragmatic competence in L2 apology. *Language Sciences*, 32, 408–424.

Chang, Y.-F. 2011. Refusing in a foreign language: An investigation of problems encountered by Chinese learners of English. *Multilingua*, 30, 71–98.

Chen, R. 2020. Single author self-reference: Identity construction and pragmatic competence. *Journal of English for Academic Purposes*, 45, 1–14.

Chen, X. and Dewaele, J.-M. 2019. The relationship between English proficiency and humour appreciation among English L1 users and Chinese L2 users of English. *Applied Linguistics Review*, 10, 653–676.

Chen, Y.-S. 2015. Chinese learners' cognitive processes in writing email requests to faculty. *System*, 52, 51–62.

Chen, Y.-S. and Lin, M.-F. 2021. Effects of peer collaboration on EFL learners' comprehension of conversational implicatures. *System*, 97, 1–12.

Chen, Y.-S. and Liu, J. 2016. Constructing a scale to assess L2 written speech act performance: WDCT and e-mail tasks. *Language Assessment Quarterly*, 13, 231–250.

Chen, Y.-S., Rau, D.-H. V., and Rau, G. (eds.) 2016. *Email discourse among Chinese using English as a lingua franca*. Singapore: Springer.

Cho, C. M. and Dewaele, J.-M. 2021. A crosslinguistic study of the perception of emotional intonation: Influence of the pitch modulations. *Studies in Second Language Acquisition*, 43, 870–895.

Cohen, A. D. 1998. *Strategies in learning and using a second language*. London: Longman.

Cohen, A. D. 2012. Research methods for describing variation in intercultural pragmatics for cultures in contact and conflict. In Félix-Brasdefer, J. C. and Koike, D. A. (eds.), *Pragmatic variation in first and second language contexts: Methodological issues*. Amsterdam: John Benjamins, 271–294.

Cohen, A. D. and Olshtain, E. 1993. The production of speech acts by EFL learners. *TESOL Quarterly*, 27, 33–56.

Cook, M. and Liddicoat, A. J. 2002. The development of comprehension in interlanguage pragmatics: The case of request strategies in English. *Australian Review of Applied Linguistics*, 25, 19–39.

Crystal, D. 1997. *The Cambridge Encyclopedia of Language*. 2nd ed. Cambridge: Cambridge University Press.

Cunningham, D. J. 2017. Methodological innovation for the study of request production in telecollaboration. *Language learning & Technology*, 21, 76–99.

Czerwionka, L. and Cuza, A. 2017. A pragmatic analysis of L2 Spanish requests: Acquisition in three situational contexts during short-term study abroad. *Intercultural Pragmatics*, 14, 391–419.

De Cristofaro, E. and Badan, L. 2021. The acquisition of Italian discourse markers as a function of studying abroad. *Corpus Pragmatics*, 5, 95–120.

Decapua, A. and Dunham, J. F. 2007. The pragmatics of advice giving: Cross-cultural perspectives. *Intercultural Pragmatics*, 4, 319–342.

Diao, W. 2016. Peer socialization into gendered L2 Mandarin practices in a study abroad context: Talk in the dorm. *Applied Linguistics*, 37, 599–620.

Diao, W. and Chen, C. 2021. L2 use of pragmatic markers in peer talk: Mandarin utterance-final particles. *IRAL*.

Economidou-Kogetsidis, M. 2013. Strategies, modification and perspective in native speakers' requests: A comparison of WDCT and naturally occurring requests. *Journal of Pragmatics*, 53, 21–38.

Economidou-Kogetsidis, M. 2016. Variation in evaluations of (im)politeness of emails from L2 learners and perceptions of the personality of their senders. *Journal of Pragmatics*, 106, 1–19.

Economidou-Kogetsidis, M. 2018. "Mr paul, please inform me accordingly": Address forms, directness and degree of imposition in L2 emails. *Pragmatics*, 28, 489–515.

Economidou-Kogetsidis, M. and Halenko, N. 2022. Developing spoken requests during UK study abroad: A longitudinal look at Japanese learners of English. *Study Abroad Research in Second Language Acquisition and International Education*, 7, 24–54.

Economidou-Kogetsidis, M., Savic, M., and Halenko, N. 2021. *Email pragmatics and second language learners*. Amsterdam: John Benjamins.

Economidou-Kogetsidis, M. and Woodfield, H. (eds.) 2012. *Interlanguage request modification*. Amsterdam: John Benjamins.

Edmonds, A. 2014. Conventional expressions: Investigating pragmatics and processing. *Studies in Second Language Acquisition*, 36, 69–99.

El-Dakhs, D. a. S. 2018. Investigating the apology strategies of Saudi learners of English: Foreign language learning in focus. *Pragmatics and Society*, 9, 598–625.

Ellis, R. 1992. Learning to communicate in the classroom: A study of two language learners' requests. *Studies in Second Language Acquisition*, 14, 1–23.

Ellis, R., Zhu, Y., Shintani, N., and Roever, C. 2021. A study of Chinese learners' ability to comprehend irony. *Journal of Pragmatics*, 172, 7–20.

Ericsson, A. and Simon, H. 1993. *Protocol analysis: Verbal reports as data*. Cambridge, MA: MIT Press.

Eslami, Z. R., Mirzaei, A., and Dini, S. 2015. The role of asynchronous computer mediated communication in the instruction and development of EFL learners' pragmatic competence. *System*, 48, 99–111.

Fakher Ajabshir, Z. 2019. The effect of synchronous and asynchronous computer-mediated communication (CMC) on EFL learners' pragmatic competence. *Computers in Human Behavior*, 9, 169–177.

Fakher Ajabshir, Z. 2022. The relative efficacy of input enhancement, input flooding, and output-based instructional approaches in the acquisition of L2 request modifiers. *Language Teaching Research*, 26(3), 411–433.

Félix-Brasdefer, J. C. 2003. Declining an invitation: A cross-cultural study of pragmatic strategies in American English and Latin American Spanish. *Multilingua*, 22, 225–255.

Félix-Brasdefer, J. C. 2004. Interlanguage refusals: Linguistic politeness and length of residence in the target community. *Language Learning*, 54, 587–653.

Félix-Brasdefer, J. C. 2008a. Perceptions of refusals to invitations: Exploring the minds of foreign language learners. *Language Awareness*, 17, 195–211.

Félix-Brasdefer, J. C. 2008b. Teaching pragmatics in the classroom: Instruction of mitigation in Spanish as a foreign language. *Hispania*, 91, 479–494.

Félix-Brasdefer, J. C. 2013. Refusing in L2 Spanish: The effects of the context of learning during a short-term study abroad program. In Martí-Arnándiz, O. and Salazar-Campillo, P. (eds.), *Refusals in instructed contexts and beyond*. Amsterdam: Rodopi, 147–173.

Félix-Brasdefer, J. C. and Cohen, A. D. 2012. Teaching pragmatics in the foreign language classroom: Grammar as a communicative resource. *Hispania*, 95, 650–669.

Fernández-Polo, F. J. 2014. The role of I mean in conference presentation by ELF speakers. *English for Specific Purposes*, 34, 58–67.

Fordyce, K. 2014. The differential effects of explicit and implicit instruction on EFL learners' use of epistemic stance. *Applied Linguistics*, 35, 6–28.

Fukuya, Y. J. and Martínez-Flor, A. 2008. The interactive effects of pragmatic-eliciting tasks and pragmatic instruction. *Foreign Language Annals*, 41, 478–500.

Furniss, E. A. 2016. Teaching the pragmatics of Russian conversation using a corpus referred website. *Language Learning & Technology*, 20, 38–60.

Gablasova, D., Brezina, V., Mcenery, T., and Boyd, E. 2017. Epistemic stance in spoken L2 English: The effect of task and speaker style. *Applied Linguistics*, 38, 613–637.

Al-Gahtani, S. and Roever, C. 2012. Proficiency and sequential organization of L2 requests. *Applied Linguistics*, 33, 42–65.

Al-Gahtani, S. and Roever, C. 2014. Preference structure in L2 Arabic requests. *Intercultural Pragmatics*, 11, 619–643.

Al-Gahtani, S. and Roever, C. 2018. Proficiency and preference organization in second language refusals. *Journal of Pragmatics*, 129, 140–153.

García García, M. 2021. Turn-initial discourse markers in L2 Spanish conversations: Insights from conversation analysis. *Corpus Pragmatics*, 5, 37–61.

García, O., Flores, N., Seltzer, K., *et al.* 2021. Rejecting abyssal thinking in the language and education of racialized bilinguals: A manifesto. *Critical Inquiry in Language Studies*, 1–26.

García, O. and Li, W. 2014. *Translanguaging: Language, bilingualism and education*. Basingstoke: Palgrave Pivot.

Garcia, P. 2004. Developmental differences in speech act recognition: A pragmatic awareness study. *Language Awareness*, 13, 96–115.

García-Gómez, A. 2020. Learning through WhatsApp: Students' beliefs, L2 pragmatic development and interpersonal relationships. *Computer Assisted Language Learning*.

García-Pastor, M. D. 2020. Researching identity and L2 pragmatics in digital stories: A relational account. *CALICO Journal*, 37, 46–65.

Gass, S. and Houck, N. 1999. *Interlanguage refusals: A cross-cultural study of Japanese-English*. Berlin: Mouton de Gruyter.

Gass, S. and Mackey, A. 2016. *Stimulated recall methodology in applied linguistics and L2 research*. London: Routledge.

Geyer, N. 2007. Self-qualification in L2 Japanese: An interface of pragmatic, grammatical, and discourse competences. *Language Learning*, 57, 337–367.

Ghavamnia, M., Tavakoli, M., and Rezazadeh, M. 2012. A comparative study of requests among L2 English, L1 Persian, and L1 English speakers. *Spanish Journal of Applied Linguistics*, 11, 105–123.

Ghobadi, A. and Fahim, M. 2009. The effect of explicit teaching of English "thanking formulas" on Iranian EFL intermediate level students at English language institutes. *System*, 37, 526–537.

Gilabert, R. and Barón, J. 2013. The impact of increasing task complexity on L2 pragmatic moves. In Mcdonough, K. and Mackey, A. (eds.) *Second language interaction in diverse education contexts*. Amsterdam: John Benjamins, 45–70.

Gilabert, R. and Barón, J. 2018. Independently measuring cognitive complexity in task design for interlanguage pragmatics development. In Taguchi, N. and Kim, Y. (eds.), *Task-based approaches to teaching and assessing pragmatics*. Amsterdam: John Benjamins, 159–190.

Glaser, K. 2016. News from the pragmatics classroom: Contrasting the inductive and the deductive approach in the teaching of pragmatic competence. *Intercultural Pragmatics*, 13, 529–561.

Golato, A. 2003. Studying compliment responses: A comparison of DCTs and recordings of naturally occurring talk. *Applied Linguistics*, 24, 90–121.

Gomez-Laich, M. P. 2018. Task complexity effects on interaction during a collaborative persuasive writing task: A conversation analytic perspective. In Taguchi, N. and Kim, Y. (eds.), *Task-based approaches to teaching and assessing pragmatics*. Amsterdam: John Benjamins, 83–112.

González-Lloret, M. 2020. Pragmatic development in L2: An overview. In Schneider, K. P. and Ifantidou, E. (eds.) *Developmental and clinical pragmatics*. Berlin: Mouton de Gruyter, 237–267.

González-Lloret, M. 2021. L2 pragmatics and CALL. *Language Learning & Technology*, 25, 90–105.

GonzáLez-Lloret, M. 2019. Task-based language teaching and L2 pragmatics. In Taguchi, N. (ed.), *The Routledge handbook of second language acquisition and pragmatics*. New York: Routledge, 338–352.

Grice, P. 1989. *Studies in the ways of words*. Cambridge, MA: Harvard University Press.

Guillot, M.-N. 2009. Interruption in advanced learner French: Issues of pragmatic discrimination. *Languages in Contrast*, 9, 98–123.

Guillot, M.-N. 2012. Conversational management and pragmatic discrimination in foreign talk: Overlap in advanced L2 French. *Intercultural Pragmatics*, 9, 307–333.

Haastrup, K. 1986. Pragmatic and strategic competence in the assessment of oral proficiency. *System*, 14, 71–79.

Habib, R. 2008. Humor and disagreement: Identity construction and cross-cultural enrichment. *Journal of Pragmatics*, 40, 1117–1145.

Haghighi, H., Jafarigohar, M., Khoshsima, H., and Vahdany, F. 2019. Impact of flipped classroom on EFL learners' appropriate use of refusal: Achievement, participation, perception. *Computer Assisted Language Learning*, 32, 261–293.

Halenko, N. 2021. *Teaching pragmatics and instructed second language learning: Study abroad and technology-enhanced teaching*. London: Bloomsbury.

Hampel, E. 2015. "Mama zimbi, pls help me!": Gender differences in (im) politeness in Ghanaian English advice-giving on Facebook. *Journal of Politeness Research*, 11, 99–130.

Haselow, A. 2021. The acquisition of pragmatic markers in the foreign language classroom: An experimental study on the effects of implicit and explicit learning. *Journal of Pragmatics*, 186, 73–86.

Hassall, T. 2003. Requests by Australian learners of Indonesian. *Journal of Pragmatics*, 35, 1903–1928.

Hassall, T. 2008. Pragmatic performance: What are learners thinking? In Alcon Soler, E. and Martinez Flor, A. (eds.), *Investigating pragmatics in foreign language learning, teaching and testing*. Bristol: Multilingual Matters, 72–93.

Hassall, T. 2012. Request modification by Australian learners of Indonesian. In Economidou-Kogetsidis, M. and Woodfield, H. (eds.), *Interlanguage request modification*. Amsterdam: John Benjamins, 203–242.

Hassall, T. 2013. Pragmatic development during short-term study abroad: The case of address terms in Indonesian. *Journal of Pragmatics*, 55, 1–17.

Hernández, T. A. 2011. Re-examining the role of explicit instruction and input flood on the acquisition of Spanish discourse markers. *Language Teaching Research*, 15, 159–182.

Hernández, T. A. and Boero, P. 2018. Explicit interventions for Spanish pragmatic development during short-term study abroad: An examination of learner request production and cognition. *Foreign Language Annals*, 51, 389–410.

Hinkel, E. 1997. Appropriateness of advice: DCT and multiple choice data. *Applied Linguistics*, 18, 1–26.

Holtgraves, T. 2007. Second language learners and speech act comprehension. *Language Learning*, 57, 595–610.

Hong, W. 2011. Refusals in Chinese: How do L1 and L2 differ? *Foreign Language Annals*, 44, 122–136.

Hosoda, Y. and Aline, D. 2022. Deployment of I don't know and wakannai in second language classroom peer discussions. *Text & Talk*, 42, 27–49.

Hudson, T. 2001. Indicators for pragmatic instruction: Some quantitative measures. In Rose, K. R. and Kasper, G. (eds.), *Pragmatics in language teaching*. Cambridge: Cambridge University Press, 283–300.

Hudson, T., Detmer, E., and Brown, J. D. 1992. *A framework for testing cross-cultural pragmatics*. Honolulu, HI: University of Hawai'i, Second Language Teaching and Curriculum Center.

Hudson, T., Detmer, E., and Brown, J. D. 1995. *Developing prototypic measures of cross-cultural pragmatics*. Honolulu: University of Hawai'i Press.

Huth, T. 2006. Negotiating structure and culture: L2 learners' realization of L2 compliment-response sequences in talk-in-interaction. *Journal of Pragmatics*, 38, 2025–2050.

Huth, T. and Betz, E. 2019. Testing interactional competence in second language classrooms: Goals, formats and caveats. In Salaberry, M. R. and Kunitz, S. (eds.), *Teaching and testing L2 interactional competence: Bridging theory and practice*. New York: Routledge, 322–356.

Hyland, K. 2019. *Metadiscourse: Exploring interaction in writing*. London: Bloomsbury.

Ishida, H. 2006. Learners' perception and interpretation of contextualization cues in spontaneous Japanese conversation: Back-channel cue *Uun*. *Journal of Pragmatics*, 38, 1943–1981.

Ishihara, N. 2019. Identity and agency in L2 pragmatics. In Taguchi, N. (ed.), *The Routledge handbook of second language acquisition and pragmatics*. New York: Routledge, 161–175.

Itakura, H. 2002. Gender and pragmatic transfer in topic development. *Language, Culture and Curriculum*, 15, 161–183.

Jaworski, A. 1994. Pragmatic failure in second language: Greeting responses in English by Polish students. *IRAL*, 32, 41–55.

Jeon, H. E. and Kaya, T. 2006. Effects of L2 instruction on interlanguage pragmatic development. In Norris, J. M. and Ortega, L. (eds.), *Synthesizing research on language learning and teaching*. Amsterdam: John Benjamins, 165–211.

Johnston, B., Kasper, G., and Ross, S. 1998. Effect of rejoinders in production questionnaires. *Applied Linguistics*, 19, 157–182.

Kang, O. and Kermad, A. 2019. Prosody in L2 pragmatics research. In Taguchi, N. (ed.), *The Routledge handbook of second language acquisition and pragmatics*. New York: Routledge, 78–92.

Kasper, G. 1997. *Can pragmatic competence be taught?*. Honolulu: University of Hawai'i, Second Language Teaching and Curriculum Center. http://nflrc .hawaii.edu/NetWorks/NW06/

Kasper, G. 2001. Classroom research on interlanguage pragmatics. In Rose, K. R. and Kasper, G. (eds.), *Pragmatics in language teaching*. Cambridge: Cambridge University Press, 33–60.

Kasper, G. 2006. Speech acts in interaction: Towards discursive pragmatics. In Bardovi-Harlig, K., Felix-Brasdefer, J. C., and Omar, A. (eds.), *Pragmatics and language learning*, Vol. 11. Honolulu, HI: National Foreign Language Resource Center, University of Hawaii at Manoa, 281–314.

Kasper, G. and Dahl, M. 1991. Research methods in interlanguage pragmatics. *Studies in Second Language Acquisition*, 13, 215–247.

Kasper, G. and Rose, K. R. 1999. Pragmatics and SLA. *Annual Review of Applied Linguistics*, 19, 81–104.

Kasper, G. and Rose, K. R. 2002. *Pragmatic development in a second language*. Oxford: Blackwell.

Kasper, G. and Ross, S. 2013. Assessing second language pragmatics: An overview and introductions. In Ross, S. and Kasper, G. (eds.), *Assessing second language pragmatics*. Basingstoke: Palgrave, 1–40.

Kasper, G. and Schmidt, R. 1996. Developmental issues in interlanguage pragmatics. *Studies in Second Language Acquisition*, 18, 149–169.

Kecskes, I. 2003. *Situation-bound utterances in L1 and L2*. Berlin: Mouton de Gruyter.

Kim, E. Y. A. and Brown, L. 2014. Negotiating pragmatic competence in computer mediated communication. *CALICO Journal*, 31, 264–284.

Kim, J. 2014. How Korean EFL learners understand sarcasm in L2 English. *Journal of Pragmatics*, 60, 193–206.

Kim, Y. and Taguchi, N. 2015. Promoting task-based pragmatics instruction in EFL classroom contexts: The role of task complexity. *The Modern Language Journal*, 99, 656–677.

Kim, Y. and Taguchi, N. 2016. Learner-learner interaction during collaborative pragmatic tasks: The role of cognitive and pragmatic task demands. *Foreign Language Annals*, 49, 42–57.

Kinginger, C. and Belz, J. A. 2005. Socio-cultural perspective on pragmatic development in foreign language learning: Microgenetic case studies from telecollaboration and residence abroad. *Intercultural Pragmatics*, 2, 369–421.

Kinginger, C. and Blattner, G. 2008. Histories of engagement and sociolinguistic awareness in study abroad. In Ortega, L. and Byrnes, H. (eds.), *The longitudinal study of advanced L2 capacities*. New York: Routledge, 223–246.

Kinginger, C. and Farrell, K. 2004. Assessing development of meta-pragmatic awareness in study abroad. *Frontiers: The Interdisciplinary Journal of Study Abroad*, 10, 19–42.

Kley, K. 2019. What counts as evidence for interactional competence? Developing rating criteria for a German classroom-based paired speaking test. In Salaberry, M. R. and Kunitz, S. (eds.), *Teaching and testing L2 interactional competence: Bridging theory and practice*. New York: Routledge, 291–321.

Koike, D. A. 1996. Transfer of pragmatic competence and suggestions in Spanish foreign language learning. In Gass, S. and Neu, J. (eds.), *Speech acts across cultures*. Berlin: Mouton de Gruyter, 257–281.

Köylü, Y. 2018. Comprehension of conversational implicatures in L2 English. *Intercultural Pragmatics*, 15, 373–408.

Kuiken, F. and Vedder, I. 2017. Functional adequacy in L2 writing: Towards a new rating scale. *Language Testing*, 34, 321–336.

Kuriscak, L. M. 2015. Examination of learner and situation level variables: Choice of speech act and request strategy by Spanish L2 learner. *Hispania*, 98, 300–318.

Labben, A. 2016. Reconsidering the development of the discourse completion test in interlanguage pragmatics. *Pragmatics*, 26, 69–91.

Lee, C. 2010. An exploratory study of the interlanguage pragmatic comprehension of young learners of English. *Pragmatics*, 20, 343–373.

Lee, C. 2016. Understanding refusal style and pragmatic competence of teenage Cantonese English learners in refusals: An exploratory study. *Intercultural Pragmatics*, 13, 257–282.

Levkina, M. 2018. Developing pragmatic competence through tasks in EFL contexts: Does proficiency play a role? In Taguchi, N. and Kim, Y. (eds.) *Task-based approaches to teaching and assessing pragmatics*. Amsterdam: John Benjamins, 137–158.

Li, C., Li, W., and Ren, W. 2021. Tracking the trajectories of international students' pragmatic choices in studying abroad in China: A social network perspective. *Language, Culture and Curriculum*, 34, 398–416.

Li, D. 2000. The pragmatics of making requests in the L2 workplace: A case study of language socialization. *Canadian Modern Language Review* 57, 58–87.

Li, E. S. H. 2010. Making suggestions: A contrastive study of young Hong Kong and Australian students. *Journal of Pragmatics*, 42, 598–616.

Li, S. 2014. The effects of different levels of linguistic proficiency on the development of L2 Chinese request production during study abroad. *System*, 45, 103–116.

Liu, B. 2016. Effect of L2 exposure: From a perspective of discourse markers. *Applied Linguistics Review*, 7, 73–98.

Liu, J. 2007. Developing a pragmatics test for Chinese EFL learners. *Language Testing*, 24, 391–415.

Long, M. H. 1996. The role of the linguistic environment in second language acquisition. In Ritchie, W. C. and Bhatia, T. K. (eds.), *Handbook of second language acquisition*. San Diego, CA: Academic Press, 413–468.

Lundell, F. F. and Erman, B. 2012. High-level requests: A study of long residency L2 users of English and French and native speakers. *Journal of Pragmatics*, 44, 756–775.

Lv, X., Ren, W., and Li, L. 2021. Pragmatic competence and willingness to communicate among L2 learners of Chinese. *Frontiers in Psychology*, 12, 1–9.

Magliacane, A. and Howard, M. 2019. The role of learner status in the acquisition of pragmatic markers during study abroad: The use of "like" in L2 English. *Journal of Pragmatics*, 146, 72–86.

Martínez-Flor, A. 2012. Examining EFL learners' long-term instructional effects when mitigating requests. In Economidou-Kogetsidis, M. and

Woodfield, H. (eds.), *Interlanguage request modification*. Amsterdam: John Benjamins, 243–274.

Al Masaeed, K. 2017. Interlanguage pragmatic development: Internal and external modification in L2 Arabic requests. *Foreign Language Annals*, 50, 808–820.

Al Masaeed, K., Waugh, L. R., and Burns, K. E. 2018. The development of interlanguage pragmatics in L2 Arabic: The production of apology strategies. *System*, 74, 98–108.

Matsumura, S. 2001. Learning the rules for offering advice: A quantitative approach to second language socialization. *Language Learning*, 51, 635–679.

Matsumura, S. 2003. Modelling the relationships among interlanguage pragmatic development, L2 proficiency, and exposure to L2. *Applied Linguistics*, 24, 465–491.

Mazzaggio, G., Panizza, D., and Surian, L. 2021. On the interpretation of scalar implicatures in first and second language. *Journal of Pragmatics*, 171, 62–75.

Meiners, J. G. 2017. Cross-cultural and interlanguage perspectives on the emotional and pragmatic expression of sympathy in Spanish and English. In Parvaresh, V. and Capone, A. (eds.), *The pragmeme of accommodation: The case of interaction around the event of death*. Cham, Switzerland: Spinger Cham, 319–348.

Miller, D., Giancaspro, D., Iverson, M., *et al.* 2016. Not just *algunos*, but indeed *unos* L2ers can acquire scalar implicatures in L2 Spanish. In Fuente, A. a. D. L., Valenzuela, E., and Sanz, C. (eds.), *Language acquisition beyond parameters*. Amsterdam: John Benjamins, 125–145.

Morkus, N. 2021. Negative pragmatic transfer and language proficiency: American learners of Arabic. *The Language Learning Journal*, 49, 41–65.

Nakamura, C., Arai, M., Hirose, Y., and Flynn, S. 2020. An extra cue is beneficial for native speakers but can be disruptive for second language learners: Integration of prosody and visual context in syntactic ambiguity resolution. *Frontiers in Psychology*, 10, 1–14.

Narita, R. 2012. The effects of pragmatic consciousness-raising activity on the development of pragmatic awareness and use of hearsay evidential markers for learners of Japanese as a foreign language. *Journal of Pragmatics*, 44, 1–29.

Newell, A. and Simon, H. 2019 [1972]. *Human problem solving*. Englewood Cliffs, NJ: Echo Point Books and Media.

Nguyen, M. T. T., Pham, H. T., and Pham, T. M. 2017. The effects of input enhancement and recasts on the development of second language pragmatic competence. *Innovation in Language Learning and Teaching*, 11, 45–67.

Nguyen, T. T. M. 2008. Criticizing in an L2: Pragmatic strategies used by Vietnamese EFL learners. *Intercultural Pragmatics*, 5, 41–66.

Nguyen, T. T. M. 2017. Using conversation tasks and retrospective methodology to investigate L2 pragmatics development: The case of EFL criticisms and responses to criticisms. *The Language Learning Journal*, 45, 399–417.

Nguyen, T. T. M. and Pham, T. T. T. 2021. L2 emails of complaints: Strategy use by low and high proficiency learners of English as a foreign language. In Economidou-Kogetsidis, M., Savić, M., and Halenko, N. (eds.), *Email pragmatics and second language learners*. Amsterdam: John Benjamins, 41–70.

Nicholas, A. 2020. Dynamic assessment and requesting: Assessing the development of Japanese EFL learners' oral requesting performance interactively. *Intercultural Pragmatics*, 17, 545–575.

Niezgoda, K. and Roever, C. 2001. Pragmatic and grammatical awareness: A function of learning environment? In Rose, K. R. and Kasper, G. (eds.), *Pragmatics in language teaching*. Cambridge: Cambridge University Press, 63–79.

Olshtain, E. 1989. Apologies across languages. In Blum-Kulka, S., House, J., and Kasper, G. (eds.), *Cross-cultural pragmatics: Requests and apologies*. Norwood, NJ: Ablex, 155–173.

Pan, P. C. 2012. Interlanguage requests in institutional e-mail discourse. In Economidou-Kogetsidis, M. and Woodfield, H. (eds.), *Interlanguage request modification*. Amsterdam: John Benjamins, 119–161.

Pérez-Llantada, C. 2014. Formulaic language in L1 and L2 expert academic writing: Convergent and divergent usage. *Journal of English for Academic Purposes*, 14, 84–94.

Plonsky, L. and Zhuang, J. 2019. A meta-analysis of L2 pragmatics instruction. In Taguchi, N. (ed.), *The Routledge handbook of second language acquisition and pragmatics*. New York: Routledge, 287–307.

Qi, X. and Lai, C. 2017. The effects of deductive instruction and inductive instruction on learners' development of pragmatic competence in the teaching of Chinese as a second language. *System*, 70, 26–37.

Qin, T. and Van Compernolle, R. A. 2021. Computerized dynamic assessment of implicature comprehension in L2 Chinese. *Language Learning & Technology*, 25, 55–74.

Qin, W. and Uccelli, P. 2019. Metadiscourse: Variation across communicative contexts. *Journal of Pragmatics*, 139, 22–39.

Reagan, D. and Payant, C. 2018. Task modality effects on Spanish learners' interlanguage pragmatic development. In Taguchi, N. and Kim, Y. (eds.), *Task-based approaches to teaching and assessing pragmatics*. Amsterdam: John Benjamins, 113–136.

Ren, W. 2013. The effect of study abroad on the pragmatic development of the internal modification of refusals. *Pragmatics*, 23, 715–741.

Ren, W. 2014. A longitudinal investigation into L2 learners' cognitive processes during study abroad. *Applied Linguistics*, 35, 575–594.

Ren, W. 2015. *L2 pragmatic development in study abroad contexts*. Bern: Peter Lang.

Ren, W. 2018a. Developing L2 pragmatic competence in study abroad contexts. In Sanz, C. and Morales-Front, A. (eds.), *The Routledge handbook of study abroad research and practice*. New York: Routledge, 119–133.

Ren, W. 2018b. Pragmatic strategies to solve and preempt understanding problems in Chinese professionals' emails when using English as lingua franca communication. *International Journal of Bilingual Education and Bilingualism*, 21, 968–981.

Ren, W. 2019a. Emancipating (im)politeness research and increasing its impact. *Acta Linguistica Hungarica*, 66, 289–298.

Ren, W. 2019b. Pragmatic development of Chinese during study abroad: A cross-sectional study of learner requests. *Journal of Pragmatics*, 146, 137–149.

Ren, W. and Guo, Y. 2020. Self-praise on Chinese social networking sites. *Journal of Pragmatics*, 169, 179–189.

Ren, W. and Han, Z. 2016. The representation of pragmatic knowledge in recent ELT textbooks. *ELT Journal*, 70, 424–434.

Ren, W. and Liu, W. 2021. Phatic communion in Chinese students' gratitude emails in English: Production and perception. In Economidou-Kogetsidis, M., Savic, M., and Halenko, N. (eds.), *Email pragmatics and second language learners*. Amsterdam: John Benjamins, 129–150.

Ren, W. and Woodfield, H. 2016. Chinese females' date refusals in reality TV shows: Expressing involvement or independence? *Discourse, Context and Media*, 13, 89–97.

Reynolds-Case, A. 2013. The value of short-term study abroad: An increase in students' cultural and pragmatic competency. *Foreign Language Annals*, 46, 311–322.

Robinson, M. A. 1992. Introspective methodology in interlanguage pragmatics research. In Kasper, G. (ed.) *Pragmatics of Japanese as native and target language*. Honolulu: University of Hawaii Press, 27–81.

Robinson, P. 2001. Task complexity, task difficulty, and task production: Exploring interactions in a componential framework. *Applied Linguistics*, 22, 27–57.

Rodriguez, S. 2001. *The perception of requests in Spanish by instructed learners of Spanish in the second- and foreign-language contexts: A longitudinal study of acquisition patterns*. PhD Dissertation, Indiana University.

Roever, C. 2004. Difficulty and practicality in tests of interlanguage pragmatics. In Boxer, D. and Cohen, A. D. (eds.), *Studying speaking to inform second language learning*. Clevedon: Multilingual Matters, 283–301.

Roever, C. 2005. *Testing ESL pragmatics: Development and validation of a web-based assessment battery*. Frankfurt: Peter Lang.

Roever, C. and Ikeda, N. 2022. What scores from monologic speaking tests can(not) tell us about interactional competence. *Language Testing*, 39, 7–29.

Romero-Trillo, J. 2019. Prosodic pragmatics and feedback in intercultural communication. *Journal of Pragmatics*, 151, 91–102.

Rose, K. R. 1994. On validity of discourse completion tests in non-Western contexts. *Applied Linguistics*, 15, 1–14.

Rose, K. R. 2000. An exploratory cross-sectional study of interlanguage pragmatic development. *Studies in Second Language Acquisition*, 22, 27–67.

Rose, K. R. 2005. On the effects of instruction in second language pragmatics. *System*, 33, 385–399.

Rose, K. R. 2009. Interlanguage pragmatic development in Hong Kong, phase 2. *Journal of Pragmatics*, 41, 2345–2364.

Ross, S. and Kasper, G. 2013. *Assessing second language pragmatics*. Basingstoke: Palgrave Macmillan.

Sánchez-Hernández, A. and Alcón Soler, E. 2019. Pragmatic gains in the study abroad context: Learners' experiences and recognition of pragmatic routines. *Journal of Pragmatics*, 146, 54–71.

Sasaki, M. 1998. Investigating EFL students' production of speech acts: A comparison of production questionnaires and role plays. *Journal of Pragmatics*, 30, 457–484.

Savic, M. 2014. *Politeness through the prism of requests, apologies and refusals: A case of advanced Serbian EFL learners*, Newcastle upon Tyne: Cambrridge Scholars Publishing.

Savić, M. and Đorđević, M. 2021. "You are the best!" relational practices in emails in English at a Norwegian university. In Economidou-Kogetsidis, M., Savić, M., and Halenko, N. (eds.), *Email pragmatics and second language learners*. Amsterdam: John Benjamins, 227–254.

Savić, M., Economidou-Kogetsidis, M. and Myrset, A. 2021. Young Greek Cypriot and Norwegian EFL learners: Pragmalinguistic development in request production. *Journal of Pragmatics*, 180, 15–34.

Schauer, G. A. 2009. *Interlanguage pragmatic development: The study abroad context*. London: Continuum.

Schauer, G. A. 2019. *Teaching and learning English in the primary school: Interlanguage pragmatics in the EFL context*. Switzerland: Springer.

Schegloff, E. A. 2007. *Sequence organization in interaction*. Cambridge: Cambridge University Press.

Schmidt, R. 1983. Interaction, acculturation, and the acquisition of communicative competence: A case study of an adult. In Wolfson, N. and Judd, E. (eds.), *Sociolinguistics and language acquisition*. Rowley, MA: Newbury House Publishers, 137–174.

Schmidt, R. 1993. Consciousness, learning, and interlanguage pragmatics. In Kasper, G. and Blum-Kulka, S. (eds.), *Interlanguage pragmatics*. New York: Oxford University Press, 21–42.

Schmidt, R. 2001. Attention. In Robinson, P. (ed.), *Cognition and second language instruction*. Cambridge: Cambridge University Press, 3–32.

Scollon, R. and Scollon, S. W. 2001. *Intercultural communication: A discourse approach*. Oxford: Blackwell.

Seedhouse, P. 2013. Oral proficiency interviews as varieties of interaction. In Ross, S. and Kasper, G. (eds.), *Assessing second language pragmatics*. Basingstoke: Palgrave Macmillan, 199–219.

Shardakova, M. 2005. Intercultural pragmatics in the speech of American L2 learners of Russian: Apologies offered by Americans in Russian. *Intercultural Pragmatics*, 2, 423–451.

Sharwood-Smith, M. 1993. Input enhancement in instructed SLA: Theoretical bases. *Studies in Second Language Acquisition*, 15, 165–179.

Shimizu, T. 2009. Influence of learning context on L2 pragmatic realization: A comparison between JSL and JFL learners' compliment responses. In Taguchi, N. (ed.), *Pragmatic competence*. Berlin: Mouton de Gruyter, 167–198.

Shishavan, H. B. and Sharifian, F. 2013. Refusal strategies in L1 and L2: A study of Persian-speaking learners of English. *Multilingua*, 6, 801–836.

Shively, R. L. 2011. L2 pragmatic development in study abroad: A longitudinal study of Spanish service encounters. *Journal of Pragmatics*, 43, 1818–1835.

Shively, R. L. 2015. Developing interactional competence during study abroad: Listener responses in L2 Spanish. *System*, 48, 86–98.

Sidnell, J. 2010. *Conversation analysis: An introduction*. Chichester, UK: Wiley-Blackwell.

Slabakova, R. 2010. Scalar implicatures in second language acquisition. *Lingua*, 120, 2444–2462.

Snape, N. and Hosoi, H. 2018. Acquisition of scalar implicatures evidence from adult Japanese L2 learners of English. *Linguistic Approaches to Bilingualism*, 8, 163–192.

Sonnenburg-Winkler, S. L., Eslami, Z. R., and Derakhshan, A. 2020. Rater variation in pragmatic assessment: The impact of the linguistic background on peer-assessment and self-assessment. *Lodz Papers in Pragmatics*, 16, 67–85.

Stavans, A. and Webman Shafran, R. 2018. The pragmatics of requests and refusals in multilingual settings. *International Journal of Multilingualism*, 15, 149–168.

Su, I.-R. 2010. Transfer of pragmatic competences: A bi-directional perspective. *The Modern Language Journal*, 94, 87–102.

Su, Y. and Ren, W. 2017. Developing L2 pragmatic competence in Mandarin Chinese: Sequential realization of requests. *Foreign Language Annals*, 50, 433–457.

Swain, M. 1985. Communicative competence: Some roles of comprehensible input and comprehensible output in its development. In Gass, S. and Madden, C. (eds.), *Input in second language acquisition*. Rowley, MA: Newbury House, 235–253.

Swain, M. 2005. The output hypothesis: Theory and research. In Hinkel, E. (ed.), *Handbook of research in second language teaching and learning*. Mahwah, NJ: Lawrence Erlbaum Associates, 471–484.

Taguchi, N. 2002. An application of relevance theory to the analysis of L2 interpretation processes: The comprehension of indirect replies. *IRAL*, 40, 151–176.

Taguchi, N. 2005. Comprehending implied meaning in English as a foreign language. *The Modern Language Journal*, 89, 543–562.

Taguchi, N. 2007a. Development of speed and accuracy in pragmatic comprehension in English as a foreign language. *TESOL Quarterly*, 41, 313–338.

Taguchi, N. 2007b. Task difficulty in oral speech act production. *Applied Linguistics*, 28, 113–135.

Taguchi, N. 2008a. Cognition, language contact, and the development of pragmatic comprehension in a study-abroad context. *Language Learning*, 58, 33–71.

Taguchi, N. 2008b. Pragmatic comprehension in Japanese as a foreign language. *The Modern Language Journal*, 92, 558–576.

Taguchi, N. 2008c. The role of learning environment in the development of pragmatic comprehension: A comparison of gains between EFL and ESL learners. *Studies in Second Language Acquisition*, 30, 423–452.

Taguchi, N. 2009a. Comprehension of indirect opinions and refusals in L2 Japanese. In Taguchi, N. (ed.), *Pragmatic competence*. Berlin: Mouton de Gruyter, 249–273.

Taguchi, N. 2009b. Corpus-informed assessment of comprehension of conversational implicatures in L2 English. *TESOL Quarterly*, 43, 738–749.

Taguchi, N. 2011a. The effect of L2 proficiency and study-abroad experience on pragmatic comprehension. *Language Learning*, 61, 904–939.

Taguchi, N. 2011b. Rater variation in the assessment of speech acts. *Pragmatics*, 21, 453–471.

Taguchi, N. 2011c. Teaching pragmatics: Trends and issues. *Annual Review of Applied Linguistics*, 31, 289–310.

Taguchi, N. 2013a. Production of routines in L2 English: Effect of proficiency and study-abroad experience. *System*, 41, 109–121.

Taguchi, N. 2013b. Refusals in L2 English: Proficiency effects on appropriateness and fluency. In Martí-Arnándiz, O. and Salazar-Campillo, P. (eds.), *Refusals in instructed contexts and beyond*. Amsterdam: Rodopi, 101–119.

Taguchi, N. 2015a. *Developing interactional competence in a Japanese study abroad context*. Bristol: Multilingual Matters.

Taguchi, N. 2015b. Instructed pragmatics at a glance: Where instructional studies were, are, and should be going. *Language Teaching*, 48, 1–50.

Taguchi, N. 2017. Interlanguage pragmatics: A historical sketch and future directions. In Barron, A., Gu, Y., and Steen, G. (eds.), *The Routledge handbook of pragmatics*. London: Routledge, 153–167.

Taguchi, N. 2019. Second language acquisition and pragmatics: An overview. In Taguchi, N. (ed.), *The Routledge handbook of second language acquisition and pragmatics*. New York: Routledge, 1–14.

Taguchi, N., Fernández, L., and Jiang, Y. 2021. Systemic functional linguistics applied to analyze L2 speech acts: Analysis of advice-giving in a written text. *New directions in second language pragmatics*. Berlin: Mouton de Gruyter, 27–57.

Taguchi, N., Gomez-Laich, M. P., and Arrufat-Marques, M.-J. 2016a. Comprehension of indirect meaning in Spanish as a foreign language. *Foreign Language Annals*, 49, 677–698.

Taguchi, N. and Li, S. 2019. Replication research in contextual and individual influences in pragmatic competence: Taguchi, Xiao & Li (2016) and Bardvo-Harlig & Bastos (2011). *Language Teaching*, 52, 128–140.

Taguchi, N., Li, S., and Xiao, F. 2013. Production of formulaic expressions in L2 Chinese: A development investigation in a study abroad context. *Chinese as a second language research*, 2, 23–58.

Taguchi, N. and Roever, C. 2017. *Second language pragmatics*. Oxford: Oxford University Press.

Taguchi, N. and Sykes, J. M. 2013. *Technology in interlanguage pragmatics research and teaching*. Amsterdam: John Benjamins.

Taguchi, N., Xiao, F., and Li, S. 2016b. Effects of intercultural competence and social contact on speech act production in a Chinese study abroad context. *The Modern Language Journal*, 100, 775–796.

Tajeddin, Z. and Alemi, M. 2014. Criteria and bias in native English teachers' assessment of L2 pragmatic appropriacy: Content and facets analyses. *The Asia-Pacific Education Researcher*, 23, 425–434.

Tajeddin, Z. and Pezeshki, M. 2014. Acquisition of politeness markers in an EFL context: Impact of input enhancement and output tasks. *RELC Journal*, 45, 269–286.

Takahashi, S. 1996. Pragmatic transferability. *Studies in Second Language Acquisition*, 18, 189–223.

Takahashi, S. 2001. The role of input enhancedment in developing pragmatic competence. In Rose, K. R. and Kasper, G. (eds.), *Pragmatics in language teaching*. Cambridge: Cambridge University Press, 171–199.

Takahashi, S. 2005. Pragmalinguistic awareness: Is it related to motivation and proficiency? *Applied Linguistics*, 26, 90–120.

Takahashi, S. 2010. Assessing learnability in second language pragmatics. In Trosborg, A. (ed.), *Pragmatics across languages and cultures*. Berlin: Mouton de Gruyter, 391–421.

Takahashi, S. 2019. Individual learner considerations in SLA and L2 pragmatics. In Taguchi, N. (ed.), *The Routledge handbook of second language acquisition and pragmatics*. New York: Routledge, 429–443.

Takahashi, T. and Beebe, L. M. 1987. The development of pragmatic competence by Japanese learners of English. *JALT Journal*, 18, 131–155.

Takimoto, M. 2008. The effects of deductive and inductive instruction on the development of language learners' pragmatic competence. *The Modern Language Journal*, 92, 369–386.

Takimoto, M. 2009. The effects of input-based tasks on the development of learners' pragmatic proficiency. *Applied Linguistics*, 30, 1–25.

Takimoto, M. 2012. Metapragmatic discussion in interlanguage pragmatics. *Journal of Pragmatics*, 44, 1240–1253.

Takimoto, M. 2020. Investigating the effects of cognitive linguistic approach in developing EFL learners' pragmatic proficiency. *System*, 89, 1–14.

Taleghani-Nikazm, C. and Huth, T. 2010. L2 requests: Preference structure in talk-in-interaction. *Multilingua*, 29, 185–202.

Tang, X. 2019. The effects of task modality on L2 Chinese learners' pragmatic development: Computer-mediated written chat vs. face-to-face oral chat. *System*, 80, 48–59.

Tang, X. and Taguchi, N. 2021. Digital game-based learning of formulaic expression in second language Chinese. *The Modern Language Journal*, 105, 740–459.

Tatsuki, D. H. 2000. If my complaints could passions move: An interlanguage study of aggression. *Journal of Pragmatics*, 32, 1003–1017.

Taylor, G. 2002. Teaching gambits: The effect of instruction and task variation on the use of conversation strategies by intermediate Spanish students. *Foreign Language Annals*, 35, 171–189.

Thomas, J. 1983. Cross-cultural pragmatic failure. *Applied Linguistics*, 4, 91–112.

Timpe-Laughlin, V. and Cho, Y. 2021. Reflecting on assessing young foreign language learners. *Language Testing*, 38, 343–355.

Timpe-Laughlin, V. and Choi, I. 2017. Exploring the validity of a second language intercultural pragmatics assessment tool. *Language Assessment Quarterly*, 14, 19–35.

Timpe-Laughlin, V., Green, A. and Oh, S. 2021. Raising pragmatic awareness: A think-aloud study. *System*, 98, 1–15.

Van Compernolle, R. A. 2013. Interactional competence and the dynamic assessment of L2 pragmatic abilities. In Ross, S. and Kasper, G. (eds.), *Assessing second language pragmatics*. London: Palgrave MacMillan, 327–353.

Vanpatten, B. 2003. *From input to output: A teacher's guide to second language acquisition*. New York: McGraw-Hill.

Vassilaki, E. and Selimis, S. 2020. Children's requestive behavior in L2 Greek: The core request. *Journal of Pragmatics*, 170, 271–283.

Verdugo, D. R. and Romero-Trillo, J. 2005. The pragmatic function of intonation in L2 discourse: English tag questions used by Spanish speakers. *Intercultural Pragmatics*, 2, 151–168.

Villarreal, D. 2014. Connecting production to judgments: T/V address forms and the L2 identities of intermediate Spanish learners. *Journal of Pragmatics*, 66, 1–14.

Walters, F. S. 2007. A conversation-analytic hermeneutic rating protocol to assess L2 oral pragmatic competence. *Language Testing*, 24, 155–183.

Walters, F. S. 2009. A conversation analysis-informed test of L2 aural pragmatic comprehension. *TESOL Quarterly*, 43, 29–54.

Walters, F. S. 2013. Interfaces between a discourse completion test and a conversation analysis-informed test of L2 pragmatic competence. In Ross, S. and Kasper, G. (eds.), *Assessing second language pragmatics*. Basingstoke: Palgrave MacMillan, 172–195.

Wannaruk, A. 2008. Pragmatic transfer in Thai EFL refusals. *RELC Journal*, 39, 318–337.

Warga, M. and Schölmberger, U. 2007. The acquisition of French apologetic behavior in a study abroad context. *Intercultural Pragmatics*, 4, 221–251.

Wei, M. 2011. Investigating the oral proficiency of English learners in China: A comparative study of the use of pragmatic markers. *Journal of Pragmatics*, 43, 3455–3472.

Wijayanto, A. 2016. Variability of refusal in L2: Evidence of L1 pragmalinguistic transfer and learner's idiosyncratic usage. *International Journal of Applied Linguistics*, 26, 99–119.

Winans, M. D. 2020. Email requests: Politeness evaluations by instructors from diverse language backgrounds. *Language Learning & Technology*, 24, 104–118.

Wong, W. 2005. *Input enhancement: From theory and research to the classroom*. New York: McGraw-Hill.

Woodfield, H. 2010. What lies beneath? Verbal report in interlanguage requests in English. *Multilingua*, 29, 1–27.

Woodfield, H. 2012. Pragmatic variation in learner perception: The role of retrospective verbal report in L2 speech act research. In Felix-Brasdefer, C. and Koike, D. A. (eds.), *Pragmatic variation in first and second language contexts: Methodological issues*. Amsterdam: John Benjamins, 209–223.

Xu, W., Case, R. E., and Wang, Y. 2009. Pragmatic and grammatical competence, length of residence, and overall L2 proficiency. *System*, 37, 205–216.

Yang, H. and Ren, W. 2019. Pragmatic awareness and second language learning motivation: A mixed-methods investigation. *Pragmatics & Cognition*, 26, 447–473.

Yang, L. 2016. Learning to express gratitude in Mandarin Chinese through web-based instruction. *Language Learning & Technology*, 20, 191–208.

Yang, L. 2019. Development of pragmatic and grammatical awareness in L2 Chinese classrooms. In Yuan, F. and Li, S. (eds.), *Classroom research on Chinese as a second language*. New York: Routledge, 190–210.

Yeh, E. and Swinehart, N. 2020. Social media literacy in L2 environments: Navigating anonymous user-generated content. *Computer Assisted Language Learning*.

Ying, J. and Ren, W. 2021. Advanced learners' responses to Chinese greetings in study abroad. *IRAL*.

Youn, S. J. 2014. Measuring syntactic complexity in L2 pragmatic production: Investigating relationships among pragmatics, grammar, and proficiency. *System*, 42, 270–287.

Youn, S. J. 2015. Validity argument for assessing L2 pragmatics in interaction using mixed methods. *Language Testing*, 32, 199–225.

Youn, S. J. 2018a. Task design and validity evidence for assessment of L2 pragmatics in interaction. In Taguchi, N. and Kim, Y. (eds.), *Task-based approaches to teaching and assessing pragmatics*. Amsterdam: John Benjamins, 217–246.

Youn, S. J. 2018b. Task-based needs analysis of L2 pragmatics in an EAP context. *Journal of English for Academic Purposes*, 36, 86–98.

Youn, S. J. 2020a. Interactional features of L2 pragmatic interaction in role-play speaking assessment. *TESOL Quarterly*, 54, 201–233.

Youn, S. J. 2020b. Managing proposal sequences in role-play assessment: Validity evidence of interactional competence across levels. *Language Testing*, 37, 76–106.

Youn, S. J. and Bi, N. Z. 2019. Investigating test-takers' strategy use in task-based L2 pragmatic speaking assessment. *Intercultural Pragmatics*, 16, 185–218.

Yousefi, M. and Nassaji, H. 2019. A meta-analysis of the effects of instruction and corrective feedback on L2 pragmatics and the role of moderator variables face-to-face vs. computer-mediated instruction. *ITL – International Journal of Applied Linguistics*, 170, 278–309.

Yuan, Z. and Zhang, R. 2018. Investigating longitudinal pragmatic development of complaints made by Chinese EFL learners. *Applied Linguistics Review*, 9, 63–87.

Cambridge Elements ☰

Applied Linguistics

Li Wei

University College London

Li Wei is Chair of Applied Linguistics at the UCL Institute of Education, University College London (UCL), and Fellow of Academy of Social Sciences, UK. His research covers different aspects of bilingualism and multilingualism. He was the founding editor of the following journals: *International Journal of Bilingualism* (Sage), *Applied Linguistics Review* (De Gruyter), *Language, Culture and Society* (Benjamins), *Chinese Language and Discourse* (Benjamins) and *Global Chinese* (De Gruyter), and is currently Editor of the *International Journal of Bilingual Education and Bilingualism* (Taylor and Francis). His books include the *Blackwell Guide to Research Methods in Bilingualism and Multilingualism* (with Melissa Moyer) and *Translanguaging: Language, Bilingualism and Education* (with Ofelia Garcia) which won the British Association of Applied Linguistics Book Prize.

Zhu Hua

University College London

Zhu Hua is Professor of Language Learning and Intercultural Communication at the UCL Institute of Education, University College London (UCL) and is a Fellow of Academy of Social Sciences, UK. Her research is centred around multilingual and intercultural communication. She has also studied child language development and language learning. She is book series co-editor for *Routledge Studies in Language and Intercultural Communication* and *Cambridge Key Topics in Applied Linguistics*, and Forum and Book Reviews Editor of *Applied Linguistics* (Oxford University Press).

About the Series

Mirroring the *Cambridge Key Topics in Applied Linguistics*, this Elements series focuses on the key topics, concepts and methods in Applied Linguistics today. It revisits core conceptual and methodological issues in different subareas of Applied Linguistics. It also explores new emerging themes and topics. All topics are examined in connection with real-world issues and the broader political, economic and ideological contexts.

Cambridge Elements ≡

Applied Linguistics

Elements in the Series

Viral Discourse
Edited by Rodney H. Jones

Second Language Pragmatics
Wei Ren

A full series listing is available at www.cambridge.org/EIAL

Printed in the United States
by Baker & Taylor Publisher Services